How to Get Published

PATRICIA W. IYER, MSN RN LNCC
President
Med League Support Services, Inc.
Patricia Iyer Associates
Avoid Medical Errors
Flemington, NJ

AL S. BROWN, PMP IPMAC
President
Real-Life Project

Patricia Iyer Associates
Flemington, NJ
www.patiyer.com

HOW TO GET PUBLISHED

Patricia W. Iyer MSN, RN, LNCC
President

Med League Support Services, Inc. — Legal nurse consulting for attorneys
www.medleague.com

Patricia Iyer Associates — Education for legal nurse consultants
www.patiyer.com

Avoid Medical Errors — Education for public about being informed patient
www.patientsafetynow.com

Al S. Brown PMP IPMA-C
President

Real-Life Projects – Consulting on project management for business
alex@rlprj.com

Publisher: Patricia Iyer Associates.
260 Route 202-31, Suite 200
Flemington, NJ 08822

Copyright 2012 by Patricia Iyer Associates

All rights reserved. No part of this publication may be reproduced, stored in a retrieval system, or transmitted, in any form or by any means, electronic, mechanical, photocopying, recording, or otherwise, without prior written permission from the publisher. This product is for sale. Purchase a copy at **www.patiyer.com**.

COLLECT YOUR VALUABLE FREE EBOOKS AT WWW.PATIYER.COM/EBOOKS.

How to Get Published: Tips from Experienced Authors

Patricia Iyer MSN RN LNCC is president of Med League Support Services, Inc., Patricia Iyer Associates, and Avoid Medical Errors LLC. Her writing for publication career began in 1979. Pat has co-authored or edited over 25 books as well as many articles, chapters, case studies and online courses. She is the author of Writing Handbook for the Legal Nurse Consultant, 2011 available at patiyer.com.

Al S. Brown PMP IPMA-C is President and Chief Safety Officer of Real-Life Projects, Inc. He has 15 years of experience in project leadership and risk management consulting, and has written and spoken actively for business audiences since 2001. You can find his speeches and articles at **http://www.alexsbrown.com**.

Purposes of the Book

Writing is a skill that can help you achieve great results in your life and career. Mastering this skill can lead to promotions, income, speaking engagements, and more opportunities than you can imagine. There are many ways you can become published today: articles, case studies, chapters, books, online courses, blogs, books, ebooks and more. The ability to reach millions of people is easier than it ever has been before. The ability to publish your own books and products is also easier than ever before.

The process of writing and being published is facilitated when you learn from those who have gone before you. In this book, we share our triumphs and hard learned lessons. This book is filled with practical content that will guide you through the process of putting together publications. Between us, we have written hundreds of articles, blog posts, case studies, online courses, chapters, and books.

You will receive practical information that you can use to get started in or improve your writing career right now. You will learn shortcuts of how to write articles, chapters and books. We go beyond the basics to the rewards of being an editor or author of a book. The content in this book is based on the realities of writing – the essentials of putting your thoughts together, working with coeditors and coauthors, and recruiting and guiding authors for a book made up of contributors.

The subject of writing for publication is broad. Here you will find guidance based on first hand extensive experience in putting together articles, chapters and books. The topics of writing for blogs, finding an agent, and marketing a self-published book are beyond the scope of this book and would fill their own books.

Welcome on your writing journey – an exciting and rewarding one. Thank you for purchasing this book. Thank you for taking this important step on your writing journey.

Pat Iyer

Al S. Brown

Table of Contents

Chapter 1 Routes into Writing 17
Pat Iyer's Story
Al Brown's Story

Chapter 2 Benefits of Being Published........................23
Time to Ask Yourself

Chapter 3 Refining Your Writing Skills......................29
Time to Ask Yourself

**Chapter 4 Three Kinds of Writing:
Exposing the Differences** 35
Academic Writing
Professional Journal or Trade Newspaper
Mass Market Publications
Comparing the Three Types of Writing
Format
References
Terminology
Are You Writing in Geek?
How to Avoid Geek
Length
Due Date
Topic
Review
Time to Ask Yourself

Chapter 5 Articles: Picking the Topic 47
Time to Ask Yourself

Chapter 6 Queries and Submission Guidelines 53

Chapter 7 One Method of Preparing an Article 59
Tips for Success
Coauthors
References
Peer Review
Time to Ask Yourself

Chapter 8 Writing a Chapter 69

Chapter 9 One Story of a Book Author 73

Chapter 10 Self-Publishing versus Signing with an Existing Publisher 81
Financial Compensation

Chapter 11 Secrets of Getting Started Writing a Book 89
Coauthors of the Book
Time to Ask Yourself

Chapter 12 Tips for Managing the Project 99
Working with the Editor
Working with Peer Reviewers' Comments

Chapter 13 Copyediting and Page Proof 107

Chapter 14 Secrets of Contributed Book 115
Formats
Picking a Topic
The Role of the Editor
Organizer

Editor as Project Manager
Recruiter
Editor as Educator
The Editor as Author
Editor as Copyeditor

Chapter 15 Tips for Working with a Coeditor of a Contributed Book 125
Chief Editor with Associate Editors

Chapter 16 Working with Authors 131
Deadlines
Unusable Material
Recruitment After the Project is Underway

Chapter 17 Revision of a Book for a New Edition ... 137
Approaching previous authors and new authors:
Sample scripts
Previous Author
Approaching New People to Co-author
New Author for New Chapter

Chapter 18 Copyright 145
Permission
The Publisher's Copyright
Use of the Material After Publication

Chapter 19 Publishing Now and in the Future 151
Trends

Appendix A Improving Your Writing Skills 155

Chapter 1: Grammar Skills............157
Abbreviations
Adverbs
Capitalization
Contractions
Dangling Modifiers
Double Negatives
Parallel Construction
Reversing the Clauses
Run On Sentences
Sic
Subject and Verb Agreement
Wordiness

Chapter 2: Punctuation 167
Apostrophes
Brackets
Capitalization
Colon
Ellipsis
Exclamation Point
Hyphen
Italics
Periods
Question Marks
Quotation Marks
Semicolon
A Love Letter.

Chapter 3: Easily Confused Words 179
Accept versus Except
Aid versus Aide
Advise versus Advice

Affect versus Effect
All right versus Alright
And/Or
And versus To
Averse versus Adverse
Because versus Since
Between versus Among
Can versus May
Cite versus Site
Classic versus Classical
Council versus Counsel
Criteria versus Data
Dependent versus Dependant
Discreet versus Discrete
Each versus Their
E.g. versus i.e.
Envelop versus Envelope
Etc.
Forward versus Foreword
Further versus Farther
Have versus Of
Insure versus Ensure
Its and It's
Lay, Laid, Lie, and Lain
Loose versus Lose
Me, Myself and I
None, Everyone, and Anyone
Personnel versus Personal
Principle versus Principal
Rational versus Rationale
Regardless versus Irregardless
Regime versus Regimen

Ruminate versus Marinate
Stationary versus Stationery
They're, Their and There
Then versus Than
Who's versus Whose
You're versus Your

Answers 191

Chapter 4: Proofreading 197

Appendix B Resources 199

Appendix C Author Guidelines 205
1. The Editors
2. Deadlines
3. Failure to Meet the Deadlines
4. Formatting
   A. Audience
   B. Confidentiality
   C. Word processor
   D. Outline
   E. First draft
   F. Manuscript preparation
      1. Headers
         a. First level header
         b. Second level header
         c. Third level header
         d. Fourth level header
      2. Synopsis
      3. Figures and tables
      4. Figure/table list

5. Endnotes and additional reading
6. Tips
7. Permissions
8. When to Send Your Files
9. Viruses
10. Important Requests

Chapter 1
Routes into Writing

Chapter 1 Routes into Writing

You may begin your writing career from several points. These could include writing an article, a book chapter, or a book that is either self-published or published by a traditional publishing house. We will cover each of these types of writing.

Pat Iyer's story

The following is Pat's story of how she got involved in writing. She always enjoyed reading books and creative writing classes she took in high school. When Pat was in graduate school, she took a course that involved bringing people with various psychological disturbances into the classroom, so that the students could interview that person and get a life story. One of the people who came in was a battered wife who had been paralyzed by her spouse. Pat was intrigued by why she stayed in that relationship and decided to do her paper for the course on the subject of domestic violence.

After Pat wrote it, the professor said to her, "This is a great paper. You ought to turn it into an article." She said, "How do I do that?" The professor explained a little bit of the process, which this book will go through.

After Pat's article was submitted and accepted, it was copyedited to the point that she couldn't turn to the article and find a single sentence that she had written. She was surprised by that and found out later that was the style of that particular journal, although, not a universal practice. It was published in 1980.

The second article that Pat wrote flowed from a paper that she presented at the American Diabetes Association Annual Conference on pregnancy and diabetes which was based on work she did in graduate school. With the encouragement of a professor, Pat submitted an abstract of a paper to present at the ADA annual conference. Pat did not fully understand this process and was so naive that she did not realize the abstract would have to be expanded into a paper to present and an article to be published. Her acceptance to give her paper led to a trip to Beverly Hills, California and publication of the article in the journal. This led to requests for columns on pregnancy and diabetes for a publication for people with diabetes.

The third article that Pat wrote was on her experiences having a premature baby. She explained the circumstances of her first son's birth and included advice to parents who were going through a similar experience. She provided advice to nurses who were taking care of such patients, and that article was accepted for publication. She has continued to write ever since. She branched out into writing books in the mid-1980s. Her first book was published in 1986. Her experience with this book is described later.

Al Brown's story

Al Brown was a reluctant writer. He studied math and sciences in high school, and only became interested in writing when he decided to start a career in business in college. He credits his English and History teachers in high school and college for giving him a solid foundation in writing and researching. Switching his major from Physics to History was an important and painful decision; math and science came easily to Al, but writing was hard for him. Fortunately, he was able to make the switch with only slight damage to his grade point average!

The first article Al wrote for a professional publication was an article on personality types for project managers. He delivered it as a speech at a local project management association meeting, and immediately saw the benefits of speaking and writing. He found that people looked at him as an authority on the topic, even though he considered himself new to the topic. Few colleagues had written about personality types, and simply capturing a few ideas and stories had a profound impact on Al's professional development. After the local meeting, his reputation and standing as a project manager grew quickly.

Al realized that his technical peers rarely spoke or published original work. Here was an opportunity to excel and stand out in his field. He quickly set up his own web site and began speaking regularly before local and international audiences. Each speech included an article – so long as he had done the hard work of researching the topic, he figured, "Why not also write an article?"

This strategy led Al to build a web site with hundreds of regular readers and over 100 articles over the following 10 years.

Chapter 2
Benefits of Being Published

Chapter 2 Benefits of Being Published

There are many benefits of being published.

a. Publications add value to your career. They may influence a hiring or promotion decision. Employees who write a chapter in a contributed book may realize increased recognition and stature in the company.

b. In academia, the "publish or perish" phrase is operative. The publication may help professors in their quest to get tenure.

c. Publications that are well done establish your credibility. You may become known as an expert in your field. Someone may say about you: "She is an expert on the subject. She wrote the book on that subject."

d. Some individuals spend their whole professional career writing articles and capitalizing on those articles in that fashion. If the publications you are writing are relevant to showing your expertise, they get you started and your name known. Your publications enable people who have interest in contacting you to find you, particularly, if the biographical information says enough about how to locate you. It is common to see an e-mail address in the biographical description which is that little paragraph at the end of the article or at the bottom of the first page of the article. It enables people to be able to reach you to ask you to speak, to consult or be involved in a project of some kind. If you are visible in other ways, an Internet search will lead people to you.

e. In comparison to writing book chapters or books, articles are faster and easier to prepare. You can move from outline to completed article in a weekend.

f. Depending on the publication, the author may receive some compensation for an article. Professional journals may pay a little; magazine with a mass circulation may buy your article for a significant sum. Books published by a traditional publisher may yield an advance or royalties. Self-published books should result in income if there are sales. No matter where you are published, remember that your ability to sell is critical to your compensation as an author. Whether you are published in a magazine or whether you self-publish, you will be responsible for generating interest and sales. One of the biggest myths in writing is the idea that an author's main role is to write the book. Most authors spend at least as much time and money marketing their work as writing it!

g. Authors may generate income in addition to royalties by buying and selling their own books. The publisher may provide a 50% discount off the retail cost of the book. The writing skills that you develop are translatable to writing in different forms such as e-books or online courses, and developing other products that can be sold to increase revenue. As long as you are comfortable with words and with the process of putting the words down on the paper, then you can publish those words in various forms.

h. An interesting article may lead to a request for you to do a column. An interesting column may be syndicated, or picked up by other publications. An interesting book or article may result in requests for more books, speaking opportunities, consulting jobs, more business, and more fame, interviews by the press, podcasts, radio shows, television shows, and more.

For example, Pat's colleague, Elizabeth Bewley wrote a book called *Killer Cure*,

Why health care is the second leading cause of death in America and how to ensure that it's not yours. Elizabeth contributes a monthly column to Pat's digital magazine, *Avoid Medical Errors Magazine*, obtainable at **www.avoidmedicalerrors.com**. Elizabeth is also the author of a weekly newspaper column called "The Good Patient." She has been interviewed by the media and gives talks about the risks of health care. It all started with her book.

Time to ask yourself

Why do you want to write?

What benefits would you derive?

Chapter 3
Refining Your Writing Skills

Chapter 3 Refining Your Writing Skills

Today, people are using very different writing styles, not just what you learned in school from your English teacher. Informal writing has changed. Text messaging, in particular, has caused us to think in terms of brevity of communication. But the real risk in brevity is that you are going to miss things and you will not be able to fully convey what you want to say, particularly within a business environment.

Getting exposed to poor writing is a big source of frustration for many people who work in professional fields. And there are errors and risks to people and to systems if we can't communicate well in terms of what we know or instructions that we need to give other people in order to be able to do their jobs well. For example, Al comments that in two areas with which he is familiar, project management and software development, he sees the impact. Some people can't express what they want. Somebody else reads unclear instructions creates a product based on those instructions.

The project may end up terribly wrong just because people couldn't express themselves.

The ability to write fluently in an easily understood manner is not going to go out of style. There are people who see typos everywhere we go and get focused on the typos and say, "Oh wait a minute, let me look at that word, it doesn't look right. Ooh, she spelled that wrong." Poor writing makes us take a few seconds away from trying to understand what we are reading in order to filter that through the editor in our minds. When writing is done beautifully, you don't notice it; when it's done poorly it jumps out and it distracts the reader from the message.

How do you improve your writing skills? One of the most important ways is to do a lot of reading of all kinds. When you are exposed to good reading material from people who understand the language and can be fluent in the language, it has a tendency to work its way into your subconscious. Look for people who have blogs about writing.

You can take a writing course or an English writing composition course, probably at a local community college or local college, or audit the course if you don't want to take it as a matriculated student if that's not congruent with your goals.

Work with somebody who has good writing skills to be a proofreader for you and a copyeditor for you to help you improve. This person will take your material and rearrange it so that it flows better. This person improves the language, grammar, and word usage.

Appendix A, at the end of the book, is designed to help you learn the basics. Refresh yourself with this information. For some of us, high school English was a long time ago and we haven't really thought about some of those things in our daily life.

It is important to remember you can always improve your writing abilities. Learn from others' writing or critiques of your writing. Develop a thick skin and graciously accept criticism so you can learn from it.

Time to ask yourself

What feedback do you typically get about your writing - clear? Could be improved? Confusing? Awkward?

What areas do you believe you need to improve?

How is your grammar, spelling, confidence about punctuation, ability to organize your material, find the right word and edit your work?

Chapter 4
Three Kinds of Writing: Exposing the Differences

Chapter 4 Three Kinds of Writing: Exposing the Differences

Consider three types of writing:

1. papers prepared in college
2. articles prepared for professional journals or specialty newsletters for a specific profession, and
3. articles prepared for a mass market magazine or newspaper.

Academic Writing

When you begin a college course, you usually find out the due dates for your papers. You may be assigned a topic or a style of writing (analysis, comparison, research). You will be given the professor's or school's preference for the layout of the paper. What style do you need to use to include references? The American Psychological Association (APA) and the Chicago Book of Style are two common ones. May you insert footnotes at the bottom of the page or may you use endnotes that appear at the end of the paper? What size margins do you need? May you submit the paper electronically to your professor or should it be on paper? The emphasis is on following the rules so that your material conforms to the school's format.

Professional Journal or Trade Newspaper

You may have a profession or trade that is served by one or more journals or trade newspapers.

Although you may not be a member of that profession, you may have specialized knowledge that is of benefit to their members. For example, you may consult on productivity in healthcare, but not be a medical professional. The editors have space to fill up, whether the publication is published in paper form or online. They may request you to submit an article. They may depend on people who volunteer to write an article, or those who submit their unsolicited manuscripts.

Journals are typically published monthly. The editors are working on an issue at least a few months ahead of its publication.

Mass Market Publications
Magazines and newspapers may be published daily to monthly. Editors may hire freelance writers to create articles about specific topics. They may invite you to prepare a column that will be recurring. Magazine editors also may rely on people who approach them with pre-written articles.

Comparing the Three Types of Writing Format
Your work may be published in paper form or online in any of these types of writing. A student may turn in a term paper in paper or send it to the professor through email or upload it onto a secure website. A professional journal or newsletter may be published in paper form or online. Some are hybrids, with a paper format that contains links to additional online articles or resources.

Magazines and newspapers may be available in paper or online forms. You may also encounter the hybrid model described above.

An article in a newspaper or magazine for the public may contain supplemental links to website content. The use of the Microsoft TagReader app at **http://gettag.mobi** or QR codes permits the publisher to take advantage of videos or additional articles on the topic. The application or code is accessed by smartphones. Download the QR code reader app from the Internet and activate it on your phone. Hold your phone up to the code to be taken to a website. You can generate your own code by doing a search for QR Code generator and using the services of the site. Save the file and insert it where you need it to go.

References

Academic writing is heavily cited. The more references, the better, according to some professors.

Articles written for professional journals are more likely to contain footnotes. However, many footnotes tend to bog down the reader. If a paper is heavily footnoted, the reader may wonder if that author said anything original or was it just a whole series of quotes from other sources. This problem may be detected when the article is submitted for publication. The author may be asked to modify the style to add more original content.

The review article is an exception to this rule. The purpose of the review article is to summarize what is known about a particular topic. For example, a physician may write a review article about the most effective ways to treat colon cancer. In the process, the author will cite many studies and research, and will usually come to a conclusion.

Articles written for the public rarely contain references. They may have links to Internet sites.

Terminology
The person reading an academic paper or professional journal can be assumed to understand common terms. The language you use is familiar to the reader. The general public reader may not be familiar with certain terms and appreciates definitions and spelled out abbreviations.

Are You Writing in Geek?
Imagine you are an attorney who has hired a legal nurse consultant to summarize and analyze complex obstetrical medical records. You don't understand medical terminology and you know that the information in the record is crucial to understanding the case. You give the records to the

nurse with the expectation that you will receive a coherent, analytical summary of the chart, a description of the standards of care, and an analysis of the deviations, if any, from the standard of care.

The legal nurse consultant submits his report, and you read this:

Assess fetus in distress via continuous electronic fetal monitoring (EFM). Evaluate FMR tracing noting:
a. Uterine activity
   1. Tachystole - hyperstimulation (>5 UCs in 10 minutes or closer than q 2 minutes)
   2. Polysystole – coupling, ineffective labor pattern
   3. Hypertonia – palpate for uterine relaxation following contraction
   4. Absence of uterine tone – uterine rupture
   5. Tetanic contractions >90 seconds long or >70 mmHg in strength (IVPC)

Huh? Geek, better known in this context as medicalese or nurse talk, is highly technical language. It is too obscure for the intended reader, in this case, an attorney. It ignores the knowledge base of the attorney and assumes a level of understanding of medical terms and abbreviations. It can result in frustration for the attorney and loss of future work for the legal nurse consultant.

This wording comes from the website of a legal nurse consultant as a sample of work product. In this example, only one abbreviation is spelled out. The terms describing abnormal labor are not all defined, and the non-obstetrical reader is left in the dark – not what you want.

How to Avoid Geek
1. Write for the reader.
2. Avoid overestimating the knowledge of your reader. Few people are offended by simple language.
3. Spell out abbreviations the first time you use them.
4. Explain complex terms the first time you use them.
5. Simplify.
6. Ask a person not in your field to read your report before you submit it. Is the material comprehensible? If not, rewrite and edit your work until it is simplified.

Length

Your professor typically gives you an expected number of pages for your paper. A publisher of a journal may specify the page length for the article. A publisher of a newspaper, for example, may tell you the expected length in words, such as 800 words.

A professor may reward you for a paper that goes into great depth and explores each nuance of a subject. A publisher of a professional journal may expect the same depth in an article, although it will be shorter than an academic paper. A professional journal article usually starts with a summary of the key points.

A publisher of a newspaper or magazine wants you to get to the point. What are your conclusions, analysis, and the pertinent facts? The reader is busy and often does not have the time to wade through volumes of material. The reader needs you to prepare a focused article, providing details, facts, and stories to illustrate the points. The tone of articles for the public tends to be conversational, whereas academic writing and professional journal styles are more formal.

Due date
A student usually starts the semester by knowing when assignments are due. Professional journals tend to have a longer review cycle after an article is submitted. You may have a sudden opportunity to submit an article for publication in a magazine or newspaper. This may require you to set aside other priorities and pour out the energy needed to complete the work. If the publisher does not provide a due date, you should ask so you can be sure to complete the work in a timely manner.

Your work may be rejected if it misses the deadline. For example, Pat hired a colleague to write test questions. When the person missed the first interim deadline, Pat called her to discuss the deadline again. She told her colleague that if the work was not submitted in time, she would not get paid. The colleague was astounded, and said, "You mean if I miss the deadline I will lose the money I would have earned?" When Pat told her, "Yes", she got the work completed in time.

Topic

College students often have a certain latitude in selecting what they will write about. The topic they pick for a term paper may be one that intensely interests them. Authors of articles for professional journals are usually quite interested in their topics and eager to share their knowledge. If you are a freelance writer for the general public, you may have little or no choice about which topic you are given to work on. Furthermore, you may have little familiarity with that subject, at least before you begin writing.

Review

Professors or their graduate student assistants read your papers and are the final decision makers about your grade, not your fellow students. A peer review process may result in your journal article being sent to people with expertise in the subject in which you have written. These reviewers provide you with ideas, suggestions, or comments about your article. They typically are "blind" reviewers, which means that they do not know your identity when they read your material. This is done to encourage objectivity.

Editors of magazines and newspapers for the public may ask others in the department to read an article submission and offer requests for changes.

Compensation

Compensation varies according to the kind of writing. You won't receive money from the professor for your paper – in fact, you paid for the right to submit it! You may receive money from a professional journal. Freelance writers are paid for their work, but other general circulation publications, (newspapers, magazines) may not provide payment. Clarify this before you begin writing. Ask, "What is your usual compensation for this type of project?"

Time to ask yourself

What kind of writing have you done?

What type of writing do you foresee doing?

What type of writing appeals to you: articles, blogs, chapters, books?

Chapter 5
Articles: Picking the Topic

Chapter 5 Articles: Picking the Topic

Let's assume you have decided to write an article. Your goal is to have it published in a professional journal, newsletter, magazine or newspaper. Here are some suggestions for getting started.

First, clearly identify your audience. Who is the primary audience? For example, you may write about leadership skills for people in the financial services industry, and the primary audience of midlevel managers. Are there any secondary audiences? Chief operating officers of the companies may be a secondary audience. Your language, stories, and examples should be geared to the audience. The more closely you can relate your material to your audience, the greater their engagement in your article.

Pick a topic that you are intensely interested in. You may be building on the article for a very long time in different forms. Your article may turn into tweets, blog posts, Facebook postings, additional articles, a chapter, and even a book. You may build on the content and become a speaker. You may be interviewed by the media because of your expertise in the subject. You never know in advance where that topic will lead you.

Pick a topic that is current and other people will be interested in. Know what the primary audience is interested in because the audiences are going to be different and the topics and what's current are going to be different as well.

How do you know what people are interested in? First, it is easiest if you know the audience. For example, if you are writing for those in health care, you should know the hot topics. In particular, there are regulatory issues that change frequently. Patient safety concepts are changing all the time. If you enjoy writing fiction, think about the type of fiction that is popular. Some authors use current headlines or stories as a springboard for their plot.

Use trends.google.com to look for mega trends. Narrow down to the country or countries you want to study. This site shows which countries search for the term you put in.

If you have targeted a particular publication or type of publication, look at the journal, newspaper or magazine and figure out what topics they typically publish. What is their focus? Are they highly technical? Do they want articles that include very specific information about finite aspects of the field? Do they publish primarily research? Or is it a broader journal that's going to appeal to a large number of people who are devoted to your area of interest?

Do a search on the Internet for websites that cover your topic. Find out how often people are searching for your specific keywords. Be specific. The subject of "management" is too broad, but "small business management" will narrow the subject.

On the other hand, you may wake up one day and get an inspiration that leads to an article. You may not know where it will get published, but feel confident you can find somebody who will be interested in this. You just start writing. There are certainly topics that can burn into you and cry out for expression. You can certainly, because you are interested in the topic, think about doing an article on it. But first, figure out before you start, who are you writing for? For example, if you are interested in time management, an article for busy parents would be written very differently than if you wrote an article for top executives, which would also be very different than if you wrote the same article for administrative assistants. These are three different groups, but they have different needs; you are going to slant the information differently.

Time to Ask Yourself

What topics interest you?

Do a keyword search for that topic at

www.goodkeywords.com
www.wordtracker.com

Put in various combinations of terms to see how many people are searching for that term- the more, the better.

Chapter 6
Queries and Submission Guidelines

Chapter 6 Queries and Submission Guidelines

Queries are used to narrow down the topic. They refer to a method of proposing the subject matter to the editor. This communication is called a query letter, although it may be as informal as a query email. Ask the editor if he or she wants an article on that topic instead of sending in an article without approaching the publisher first. The publisher may have just accepted or published another article on the same topic.

You will find out if the editor has an interest in the subject. Some subjects are "evergreen", such as how to lose weight, whereas others may be seasonal. An article on how to prepare a holiday meal may be relevant only at a certain time of the year.

Other topics may have many facets. To take a patient safety example, there are so many aspects of trying to make health care safer that you can literally never run out of material.

Professional journals may publish articles on such limited topics that it is clear that the audience is limited. For example, a physician may write about the intestine of the mouse and the enzymatic processes involved in digestion.

In some fields, it is also important to keep in mind that your proposals should go to only one publisher at a time and if that publisher says, "Yes, I want that article", it's not appropriate to take that same concept and submit it to another publisher simultaneously. That has occurred particularly in the nursing world and Pat is familiar with at least two instances that occurred in the last decade. That may not seem like a lot but it's tremendously embarrassing to the publishers to have their rival publication come out with the same article, the same month, on the same topic, by the same authors. And those authors can expect that it's going to be hard for them to have articles accepted in the future at least by those journals. So, it's a big black mark for the author.

In other fields, such as project management, it is possible to get the same article published in multiple places as long as the author tells them, "This was already published in this other journal." The article could have been originally published in a regional journal that provides content specific to a state. The article could be refocused to a different topic area but the article is still relevant. Approaching the publisher and being forthright avoids an awkward situation.

Remember that the editor has empty space to fill up in each publication issue. He or she needs content and you need or want to be published. So the publishers are often in that "I'm hungry, feed-me" mode. They welcome ideas and articles, particularly, if they are going to fit the needs of their audience. The topic must be relevant and the material submitted in a timely fashion.

Be sure to find out about the publications submission guidelines. Either look at a back issue of a journal or magazine, the publication's website, or request information on the publication's submission guidelines. Editors may be overjoyed you took the time to ask. Many authors submit unsolicited articles; they don't meet the requirements and so on. It is a chore to go through these bad articles.
If you ask ahead of time, the editors are very happy.

It saves everyone a lot of time.

Submission guidelines are not uniform. They are specific to each publication, in terms of the margins and how the footnotes should be handled. It's important to follow those. They are there for a reason. And it does make it easier for the publisher to get a submission that conforms to their guidelines by somebody who has taken the time to look up that information.

Do not fall prey to the myth that if you want to publish an article, that you have to be somehow inspired first. Do not believe there is no way to work into this. You can do the work; you can figure out your market. You can research the publications and if you are determined you can be a successful published author. It's not all inspiration.

Once you've published once with a publication, it becomes a little bit easier to get published a second time, assuming you have new, unique, interesting content that's relevant to them.

Chapter 7
One Method of Preparing an Article

Chapter 7 One Method of Preparing an Article

It is important not to be intimidated by the writing process. Everyone starts at the same place, having not had anything published before. Do your research, and know about the journal, the magazine, the newspaper, and whatever audience you've decided you want to write for to make sure it's a good match with what you want to say. If you know the style of the journal or magazine in advance that helps to determine if this is a topic that you think this particular journal is going to be interested in.

Here is a step by step process.

1. Set up a file folder or file folders. Gather information. These may be in the form of articles, chapters, online sources, and so on.
2. Develop an outline. Number each point in the outline.
3. Go through your sources. Read them again and put a number at the top of the source that corresponds to the number on the outline.
4. Review your outline again to see if you need to gather any additional information to fill in gaps.
5. Begin with the first point. Gather all the materials that have number one on them, for example. Look for the key points that you

want to include and then write that section of the article. Move on to the second point.
6. By the time you are done, you will have used most of your resources. You may determine in re-reading your references that some do not fit into the outline. Either modify the outline or set them aside.
7. Set the article aside for at least a couple of days and go back to it and then read it again to see if it's coherent. Do some fine-tuning or editing.
8. Misspellings, typos, incorrect punctuation, and a disorganized report reflect haste and lack of effort. Create the most effective article you can. Your reputation depends on it.
9. After spell checking, proofread by printing out the document and reading it line by line. Use a red pen to make it easier to spot the changes so you an input the changes on the computer.
10. Read the text out loud. Read what is on the page, not what you expect to see. Listening to your sentences will help you identify errors or awkwardly phrased sentences.
11. Ideally, proofreading should be done after a day has passed to allow you to read the document with a fresh eye.
12. Look for the types of errors you typically make. Double check for these. Common errors not picked up by the spell checker are "form" versus "from", "tot he" instead of "to the", and "trail" versus "trial". If you know you tend to make common errors of this

nature, insert the word into the autocorrect feature, and add an asterisk after the word. For example, replace trail with trial*. The asterisk will catch your eye as you proofread and prompt you to verify you've used the correct word.

13. Look for one of a pair that is missing, such as the second quotation mark or parenthesis.
14. Proofread for typos, for consistency, and for logical arrangement of information.
15. Ask another person with good proofreading skills to read your work. This individual will often find errors your eye has skipped over.
16. If you are interrupted when inputting changes into the computer, place highlighting on the section of the report where you stopped. The highlighting will make it easier to resume in the correct spot.
17. Examine all aspects of the document, including headers and footers, and the name and address of the person to whom a letter is addressed. Pat's last name has been spelled Iyre, Ilyer, Iyers, Ayre, and Tyer. The spelling she is least fond of is "Lyer".
18. Activate readability statistics on your word processor. Check the Flesch Kincaid Score after you finish proofreading. This is roughly equivalent to grade level. If you write for the general public, strive to keep the level at 8 or below. Professionals may read at the 10th level. Try to avoid a score much higher than that. You can reduce the score by making

your sentences shorter and using fewer multi-syllable words.
19. Minimize your use of passive voice. Passive voice involves writing sentences in a stilted way: "He was taken to the store. He was given medication." The person performing these actions is not identified. You can rewrite these sentences: His sister took him to the store. The pharmacist gave him the medication." Strive to keep your percent of passive voice sentences to less than 10 percent.

Tips for Success
Coauthors

If you are working with other co-authors, divide up the work among the two or the three or how many other people you are involved with. It also makes it easier in some senses to get started on your article because you have got somebody else's perspective. We all have an ego at times that leads us to believe that whatever we have put together is perfect and doesn't need to be changed. But it's important to bounce your ideas off somebody else. You want a person who is going to give you honest feedback. The product will be stronger because you are putting your combined ideas together.

References

Use of footnotes or endnotes makes citing references infinitely easier than typing in numbers after each referenced piece of text. The automatic renumbering feature of endnotes prevents you from getting citations out of sequence. However, Microsoft Word endnotes and footnotes do not translate well in some desktop publishing programs or to Macintosh operating systems.

There are a few ways around this. First, do not use a lot of references. It is far easier to manage a few than many. Second, use endnotes when preparing the article, and then bookly switch them to large numbers. This is how you do it:

1. Use the references feature of your word processor to keep your numbers in order. The beauty of this feature is that as you add new references, the numbers automatically change to accommodate the new reference. However, if your publisher cannot accept the manuscript with the references, you'll have to change them.
2. After you have finished inserting reference numbers, save your file. Always save a copy of the original work before you start altering endnotes. Rename the file as something different.
3. If you remove an endnote number from the body of the material, the citation will disappear at the end of the article. Find the first citation, which will have a superscript number. After the number, type a large number. For example, your sentence would look like this. [1]
4. Copy and paste the endnote into a new document. When you have typed large

numbers after all of the superscript ones, and have copied all of your endnotes onto a separate document, go back to delete the superscript numbers in the manuscript.
5. Another way to do this is to not use the reference feature. Keep two documents open: the article and a document for the references.
6. Whenever you cite a source, place the reference in the second document. This method requires you to watch your numbering to keep it in order. It is easy to get the numbers out of order.
7. Dual monitors make this process easier, if your computer will accommodate a second monitor.

Peer Review

The editors of professional journals that are "peer reviewed" send out an article for a blind peer review. It goes to two or three people who the editor has selected as experts in the field to review your material to make sure that it's accurate, current, and pertinent to the audience.

The reviewer is typically given a standard form to fill out and asked to answer questions about whether this particular article is worthy of being published. The reviewers add additional comments about the article. They may suggest changes such as refocusing the content. When the article comes back to you from the publisher, you might get a summary of their comments, or you might get their actual comments. You will get a decision from the publisher about whether your material is something they want to publish. The journals that have the peer review process are considered to be more reputable than the ones that don't have that process and it helps to provide some level of assurance to the publisher that the material is worthy and should be included in the journal.

Time to Ask Yourself

Have you used references in your writing?

Have you activated readability statistics? Check your Help feature to see how to do this on your word processor.

Chapter 8
Writing a Chapter

Chapter 8 Writing a Chapter

Someone may approach you to contribute a chapter to a book. First, acknowledge the honor that someone had confidence in you to ask you to contribute. Here are some questions to ask:

1. What is your format? Do you have a sample chapter you could send to me?
2. What is your deadline?
3. Who is the audience for this book?
4. Has this book been published before?
5. What other chapters do you plan for the book and how will mine fit in?
6. Do you need an outline first?
7. Do you want a first draft in rough or near final form?
8. What is the expected length?
9. In what form do you want me to turn over the material?
10. Do you have a form you want me to use to obtain permission to reproduce something in the chapter?
11. When do you expect the book to be published?
12. Is there compensation for being involved in this book?
13. What can I do to help you publicize the book?

Writing a chapter is like writing a long article. The tips for writing an article apply. The chapter is typically written in stages:

1. Develop an outline.

2. Collect your sources.
3. Organize them according to your outline.
4. Write your first draft. Do not attempt to edit it while the creative thoughts are flowing. Your objective is to get your ideas written down.
5. Set aside time to chip away at your chapter. Avoid waiting until just before it is due – you may run out of time.
6. Format your first draft according to guidelines given to you by the publisher or editor. If you are self-publishing the book in which the chapter appears, set up a uniform format for sizes of fonts for headers.
7. Submit the first draft to your editor. Assume that most editors do not want to see a rough draft, but something that is as close to done as possible.
8. Wait for feedback from your editor, while continuing to be alert to sources of additional information about your topic.
9. Refine your second draft using the feedback you've been given.
10. Adhere to all deadlines. Later in this book, you will see the problem of missed deadlines from the perspective of the editor.

Chapter 9
One Story of a Book Author

Chapter 9 One Story of a Book Author

This is Pat's story of her first book: I was working with two other people on a self-learning module which was geared towards teaching nurses about the nursing process. The nursing process is a very basic problem solving part of nursing practice. The three of us put together the self-learning module to teach the nurses in our respective hospitals about this topic. When we were done we said, "We ought to try to get this published." We knew that we had put together material that would be useful to the nursing profession. We wanted to share that information that we had assembled so laboriously. At this point in my career as well as the careers of the other people, we were looking ahead and thinking about where this could take us. We had no idea where it would, but it just seemed like it needed to be done.

We decided to approach a major nursing publisher. We didn't look at the holdings of each of the publishers. We knew that they were nursing publishers; we didn't know if they had anything else on the topic. It was as unscientific as that.

In our innocence, we thought they would take our work as it was. We sent in the self-learning module and asked if the publisher was interested in publishing it as it was. The response that we got back was "No, we are not interested but you really need to turn it into a book. It needs to be fleshed out. It's too much of a skeleton outline." We rejected this idea as too much work. Then we went to another major nursing publisher and asked the same question and the response was "No, we are not interested in publishing it as it is, we really think it needs to be fleshed out and turned into a book." The second time we heard that we decided that we would follow the publisher's advice.

After the second publisher showed interest, we received a lot of paperwork that asked us for a proposal. These were the kinds of questions:

- Who is the book geared to?
- What is the intended outline of the content?
- How many chapters are you envisioning?
- What are the competing books?
- Have you done your research and found out what else is out there on the market on your topic?
- How is your book going to be different than those books?
- Can you send us a sample chapter?

We followed the process of completing the book proposal and sample chapter, and the proposal was accepted. We were then asked to come to Philadelphia, the location of the publisher. This was WB Saunders, which now has been taken over by another publishing company. We were taken into the library of the publishing company. It was a very awe-inspiring experience to go into this library to sign the publishing contract because the library had copies of all of the books that WB Saunders had ever published. It was this large room lined with book shelves and we realized that our book was going to be up on one of those shelves one day.

We were practically floating when we walked out. We went back toward the car. The two of us were just chattering away – so excited, and so honored to have signed this publishing contract. There was a man on the sidewalk ahead of us who turned sideways and undid his pants and dropped his pants to his ankles and he was not wearing any underwear. The two of us in unison turned around and walked in the opposite direction and it brought us down to earth immediately. That was my most memorable book proposal signing experience.

The other peak experience that we had associated with that book was it was released directly to a nursing diagnosis conference in St. Louis. It was sent right from the printers to the conference. The publisher got the crates of books and set them up with the booth to start selling them. The publisher began selling them before we had seen the first copy of the book. As my co-authors and I were walking through this mall in St. Louis on the way to the convention we passed a woman who was holding our book in her arms. We instantly wanted to grab and her say, "You bought our book. Look, look there it is." It was thrilling to us to see her carrying it.

This book went through its first edition and at that time the publishers were using a guideline that if a book was about 5 years old, it would be considered to be too dated. At the end of about 4 years the publisher came to us and said, "It's time to revise this book for another edition." It went through a second edition; we added more chapters; we expanded the material; we updated it. It went through a third edition after another 5 years. It went through a life-span of about 15 years and it got translated into Spanish, Portuguese, and Japanese. When it was time to do the fourth edition, the three of us were all doing different things and away from what we had been doing at the time that we started working on the book. So we decided at that point to let it go.

    The Spanish edition resulted in an invitation for me to teach in Spain. I got invited to Pamplona in Spain to speak to the school of nursing in a continuing education conference on the topic of the nursing process. I went in there with one set of ideas in my mind in terms of how to approach the material but then spent two days on tour, getting to know the people. By the time I taught, my ideas about what I wanted to present had turned 180 degrees in a different direction. If I hadn't had the book published in Spanish, and hadn't had that invitation, I never would have had an opportunity to go through seeing Pamplona and the experience of teaching in another country.

    My first several books were written for the nursing audience. I wrote with my two co-authors about the nursing process and nursing diagnosis. Next, I wrote a book about nursing documentation. In subsequent editions, I added other nursing authors to expand the content. A publisher approached me about being the editor of books on care planning. I recruited three authors and developed a series of three books of care plans.

By the time the care plan books were being written, I was working with attorneys who handled medical malpractice and personal injury cases. One day in themed-1990s, when I was exhibiting for my business at a large conference for plaintiff attorneys, another exhibitor approached me about editing a book on nursing malpractice. He was an author and editor for a legal publisher, and knew they were looking for someone to assemble a book on nursing malpractice. I spoke to the publisher and agreed to do it. That book is currently in its fourth edition. Since that day, I have edited or coedited a book on medical records (in its second edition), a book on medical legal aspects of pain and suffering, and a book on nursing home litigation.

During my president elect year while serving on the board of directors of the American Association of Legal Nurse Consultants, I was asked to be the chief editor of the Principles and Practices of Legal Nurse Consulting. This involved recruiting and training associate editors, determining what content needed to be changed, deleted or added to this second edition, and editing the material that our authors wrote. A few years after this book was completed, I acted as chief editor for a smaller book on business principles of legal nurse consulting. Two associate editors worked with me on that project.

My publishing experience also involves self-publishing. I have created books that are spiral bound, and books that are printed by a print on demand publisher.

It seems that I write all of the time now. I maintain four blogs for four different sites, write an ezine for my list of subscribers, and edit articles for Avoid Medical Errors Magazine. Get details about the magazine at **www.avoidmedicalerrors.com** or scan the QR code with your smart phone.

I love to write and help others improve their skills.

Chapter 10
Self-Publishing versus Signing with an Existing Publisher

Chapter 10 Self-Publishing versus Signing with an Existing Publisher

A basic decision that has to be made is whether or not you want to approach an existing publisher or you want to self-publish. Self-publishing has greater opportunities for you having control over the project and certainly greater possibilities of financial reward if the book does well. It also requires more money upfront in terms of putting the project together, getting it printed and then there is the whole question of how you distribute this book. Many authors are successful promoting their books through tweeting, blog posts, speeches, ads, book launches, and so on.

Self-published books may have anywhere from the most casual to the most polished of appearances. You can self-publish a book and take it to an office supply store and have it bound with wire or with plastic comb and that's a self-published book. You can set up your own self-publishing company and call it Alex Brown Incorporated or Brown Publishing or any topic, any name that you want to give it as long as it's not taken by somebody else.

You can also self-publish your book and put it out in an e-book format so that there is no physical book, but a downloadable PDF file that you sell. There are print-on-demand publishers who will create one copy of a book for you, which you can customize for a particular audience or client. We use CreateSpace, a branch of Amazon.com.

You can go to a company that will charge you money to publish your book. The term in the publishing industry is a "vanity press". Many of those self-published books end up not selling well because the other part of the equation is how do you distribute the book? You might get a 100 or 1,000 copies that sit in your garage but unless you have a mechanism for getting that book in the hands of other people, such as a website or fliers or word of mouth, then you have just put a lot of money into the project and not seen any return.

It is very difficult to get a self-published book into a standard book store. They tend to want to accept just the books from the major houses. Keep this in mind when you make a decision to self-publish. The marketing and promoting of the book will determine its success.

In one way it's easier to start with an existing publisher because you learn the process; you learn how to look at the market and think about how your book is different than other competitors. You learn the process of putting together the outline; you learn the benefit of having somebody else as a copyeditor. Typically, the publisher will assign somebody to go through the manuscript and you learn the manuscript lingo language – the little copy editing symbols that a copyeditor uses. You have somebody who will take over the distribution of the book. Of course, as an author you don't get a 100 percent of the money. You might get 10 to 12 to maybe 15 percent of the money that comes in from selling that book. The publisher is taking the risks.

When you sign up with a major publishing house, one of the advantages is you have professional editors who are people on salary, who will pull you towards the goal of actually publishing that book. If you self-publish, you have to push other vendors towards your goal of publishing that book. So it depends on your experience and what you are hoping to get out of the result.

On the other hand, the bar to getting published by a conventional publisher is high. Many publishers are deluged with manuscripts and they are averse to taking risks. They are most interested in authors who have platforms – a proven track record in selling their own self-published books, or a speaking schedule, for example, that will generate large sales. The publisher may ask the author to contribute dollars towards marketing.

Another trend is to ask the author to buy a quantity, such as 5,000, of his books at a discount. This shifts the risk of publishing from the publisher to the author. This type of proposal has to be very carefully considered because the financial outlay can be significant. For example, a book that would sell for $20 would be purchased by the author at a 60% discount or for $12. A requirement to buy 5,000 copies would mean an outlay of $60,000. An author who self-published a book and printed on demand would pay about $5 for the same book, and would have no minimum purchase requirement.

See **Appendix B** for some resources if you are interested in the self-publishing route.

Financial Compensation
Let's talk more about the money aspects of writing a book. Is this a way to get rich? We read about these amazing authors who make a lot of money. Is writing books a money making tool? Can you write books and just sit back and let the royalty checks come in? The answer is "rarely". It's important to understand the term "mass market". Mass market means that the books are being written for the general public and are available in convenience stores on a book rack and a book store chain or online site. People by the hundreds of thousands are buying them. If you are writing in a specialized technical area, you may not be able to sell thousands of books.

The book is typically priced by the publisher based on his knowledge of what the market will bear. If you are going with a conventional publisher, recognize that the royalties are probably not going to exceed about 15 percent. Typically it's on a sliding scale, so that the first 10,000 books, for example, might result in royalties of 10 percent. Then between 10,001 copies up to 15,000 copies there might be a bump up of royalties of 12 percent. After 15,000 copies, it might get up to 15 percent. These numbers are highly variable. The more you sell, the higher percentage you get in terms of royalties, but you hit a ceiling. The publisher needs the bulk of that money to pay for overhead. If you work with a publisher or you are writing an article you are not necessarily going to be able to sit back and retire on that money.

If you are doing a self-published book then you need the vehicle to be able to go out and market the book. If you are speaker, for example, you could potentially make a lot of money selling your own book in the back of the room, through an arrangement with the program sponsor that each attendee gets a book, or selling it on your website.

People who are self-publishing are not sitting back and letting the money roll in. They are doing a lot of work to market that book, whether it's through speaking, developing websites, or other businesses that create book sales. There is rarely any easy money in writing.

A hybrid model of self-publishing in combination with a traditional publisher may result in a nice income. Sometimes authors put out a book through a traditional publisher from whom they get only a small portion of royalties but then they self publish something like a work book, information sheets, DVDs or audio products that go along with the book. Sometimes they make more money off of the add-on product than they would on the original book.

New ways of making money through writing are created and destroyed every year. Years ago, people made money selling pamphlets through classified ads in local newspapers. Many "how to" books were self-published and marketed this way. Now the Internet has replaced classified ads, and authors are making money selling similar material on-line. Some authors make money on "pay per click" ads that appear on their own web sites. Other authors partner with specific companies and earn commissions for promoting sales of related products. The only limit to the ways that you can earn money on your self-published material is your imagination!

Chapter 11
Secrets of Getting Started Writing a Book

Chapter 11 Secrets of Getting Started Writing a Book

How do you begin the process? Does it seem daunting to try to put together 100 pages or 200 pages? The most important thing is to look at your topic and see how it can be broken down. The first step is to come up with the outline of the chapters. If you know the focus of the book, and you know what you want to cover, then the material divides itself up. You are probably going to have an introductory chapter and then you are going to go into the content of the book. There is no magical number in terms of how many chapters you have. As you write, you will see ways to add additional chapters, or combine two chapters into one.

Begin collecting your material as you do for an article; look at your sources. Develop an outline. If you follow the system described above for articles, you assign numbers to your sources, so that you can write based on your outline.

Another way to get started is to assemble articles you have written. First, be sure you have not turned over the copyright to the publisher of the article. If you have, plan on making extensive changes to the material so that it becomes new.

Take your blog posts and sort them into categories. If you use Word Press as your platform, and have kept up with categorizing each post, this should be easy. Is there overlap, redundancy, or outdated material? Set those aside. Next, assemble the blog posts into categories and add in any articles you may have written about the topic. Determine if you have enough to fill a chapter, however you define "enough". Determine if the material needs to be supplemented with an introduction to each chapter, additional content, and a conclusion. Think in terms of adding an introductory chapter or a foreword. A book made out of blog posts is a "blook".

Another way to create a book is to take transcripts of teleseminars or webinars and weave them together. You could also have someone interview you, record the conversations, and edit the transcripts to turn them into a manuscript. In fact, this book you are reading started as a transcript of an interview between Al Brown and Pat Iyer. We edited and expanded upon the transcript. Typically, we are colloquial when we talk. The editing removes the informality of the language and also takes out extraneous words, like "Well" at the beginning of a sentence or "um".

You have the option of hiring a person to write the book for you or with you. A ghostwriter is a person who writes the book and is not credited as the author. This is work for hire. Such people may be located in your network or online at sites like **www.elance.com** or **www.guru.com**. Ask to see samples of the person's previous writing. Look at rating provided by other people who have hired this individual. Is English the person's first or second language? If possible, narrow down the search of a few people and compare what they have to offer. Consider giving a limited assignment to see how the person does before turning over the whole project. Pay the author upon delivery of the work, not before.

Pat has hired freelance people for two projects. Based on analysis of the most frequently visited page on her site, she hired a person to write an ebook on the topic. Pat edited the material and added to it. The project turned out well and is making a profit.

In the second project, Pat gave the freelancer transcripts of webinars. The freelancer rewrote the transcripts to take out the dialogue, added two more chapters, and did a beautiful job. This book was published through CreateSpace.

Add links to videos in a book to create a "vook". It has content interspersed with links.

Coauthors of the Book

Should you have a coauthor for your book? There are advantages and disadvantages. The advantages:

- The coauthor may have different knowledge than you do about the subject, thus enabling you to expand the content.
- The coauthor who is a good editor will be able to edit your material to improve word flow and pick up typos.

- The project may be completed more quickly if you are both writing simultaneously.

Pat wrote her first book with two coauthors. One lived close to her. They got together on weekends several times over the course of the project to discuss content, review what each other had written, and plan the course of the other chapters. Her coauthor was able to see ways to improve the material, and it was a valuable collaboration.

Disadvantages of coauthoring the book include:

- A coauthor who does not follow through with commitments can create much frustration and even derail the project.
- Coauthors may not be matched in skill level, which can affect the success of a project that relies on each author having approximately the same level of writing and editing skill.
- Coauthors may disagree on perceptions of who did more work on the project and on how to split the royalties.
- Coauthors may not have the same ability to promote the book or be jealous of publicity the other author receives.

Pat recalls her coauthor was upset when Pat's employer put a notice in the newspaper when her first book was published. The announcement did not list all three coauthors' names, a fact over which Pat had no control.

When looking for a coauthor, select someone you know well. You need someone who will hold up his or her end of the bargain. Pick someone who is responsive and dedicated to the project. Pat recalls a coauthor who stopped returning phone calls towards the end of the project. The coauthor was responsible for sending the manuscript to the publisher, which she did by regular mail two weeks before Christmas. The box never made it to the publisher. The publisher kept calling Pat looking for the box, and Pat kept calling her coauthor, who did not return calls. Then Pat copied the coauthor on a letter to the publisher referring to the missing box. At this point, three months later, the coauthor finally realized the manuscript did not arrive at the publishers. Valuable time was lost.

Today authors can submit their chapters electronically (via email) or load onto a cloud site, such as dropbox.com or box.net. When paper needs to be returned to the publisher, authors should use a secure delivery method, such as Fed Ex or UPS.

Pick a co-author who will put in the effort needed to create the product. You should have a frank discussion about time commitments and rearrangement of priorities to accommodate a writing schedule. Anticipate problems that might occur and discuss how you would handle them. What will happen if one author cannot continue on the project? Whose name will appear first? Recognize that the book may become known by the name of the first author, rather than both of you or all three of you. Will this make the other authors jealous?

Publishing contracts mandate that you define how much percent each author will earn in royalties. When you work with a traditional publisher, these issues have to be discussed in the beginning in order for all individuals to be able to start the project.

It is important to decide upfront how you will divide the work and the compensation. If you have three people for example, then you have to decide, is each person going to be able to contribute an equal amount or are two people or one person going to be doing more of the project? For example, one of the individuals may know that life circumstances will prevent an equal division of work, and will accept a lesser royalty. For example, the coauthors of Pat's first book split the royalties 40-40-20 because one coauthor knew she could contribute much less.

Without a clear discussion in the beginning, some co-author relationships can go very poorly when they do not discuss these issues until the very end. This may result in a lot of disputes over who wrote how much and how they should split royalties.

If you have gone through a contract phase with a traditional publisher, you will know that these issues need to be brought up in the beginning. If you are inexperienced when you self-publish, you could leave those kinds of questions to the very end. If you are working with an established publisher, they will ask you to settle those issues upfront because they know they are going to be difficult.

Pat recalls asking a colleague to update a book she wrote for expert witnesses. This individual was committed to teaching several programs with Pat over the course of several months. Pat did not define how the sales of the book would be split, thinking that would be determined when she saw how much work her colleague put into updating the book. Her colleague seized the opportunity to completely rewrite the book and then said it was now hers and she would sell it at the programs.

When Pat told her that she did not intend to lose her work product, her colleague told her she made a business decision.

At that point, Pat talked to an attorney, who said it would cost more in intellectual property attorney fees to dispute the issue than the book would generate. So Pat and her colleague each sold their books at the programs. This incident fouled their relationship and made teaching the programs difficult at best.

Time to Ask Yourself
Do you want to write a book?

What topic would you select?

Do you have someone in mind for a coauthor?

Chapter 12
Tips for Managing the Project

Chapter 12 Tips for Managing the Project

We discussed in the previous chapter about how writing takes time. We have all got jobs; we've all got families. How do you manage to find the time and have the discipline to write a book, while all these other things are still going on in your life? You have to make the time if it's something that's important to you. In the beginning, it's important to talk to your family about the fact that you want to do this and that it's going to change some things. It sometimes requires role changes. Sometimes a spouse may have to do things that are not ordinarily considered part of his or her job description. And that's why you see in so many books a dedication, "To my loving husband who tolerated and put up with this project"- words to that effect. Because it does require changes and if you try to do everything in your life that you have been committed to and write the book, then you end up short changing yourself in some way.

What are you willing to give up to complete the project? Is it watching movies or TV, taking your child to soccer games, or being involved in a professional association?

Pat recalls a coauthor who could not give up anything in her life when she was coauthoring their book. Consequently, she was often late or missed deadlines. She did not realize that she had to reorganize her priorities.

Recognize that you are likely going to be giving up free time for an extended period in order to be able to get this project accomplished. You may be a person who can get up every day at 4 AM and write for three hours. Or you may be a person who can put together a book by dictating it over the course of many weekends. It would be unusual to be able to write a book in one weekend unless you are extraordinarily focused and have all of your sources lined up ready to go, and it is a short book.

Working with the Editor
Each traditional publisher tends to follow a set of guidelines for manuscript production. They do this to provide a consistent look to their publications. The guidelines are laid out in a manuscript or book. It is very important to thoroughly read these guidelines before starting the writing process. It will save enormous amounts of hours if the material is prepared to conform to the publisher's requirements. They require that references, for example, follow a specific format. It would require many hours of extra work to take a heavily referenced manuscript and revise the references to fit the format. You don't want to have to do that.

Traditional publishers employ editors and copyeditors. The editor is involved in recruiting authors for books, reviewing book proposals, and guiding the project. Some may ask to review the manuscript at stages, whereas others may wait until it is completed. Typically what happens is that after the book proposal is accepted, the publisher doesn't really want to see those chapters until they have been finished in what you would consider their final form. This person is a resource when there are issues that come up.

Communication with the editor is important but be aware that this can also add a lot of time to the writing process. Pat learned a lesson in her first book. She was spending a lot of time on the phone with her editor on work time. Although she thought that was kind of invisible to the people working in her department of the hospital, it was definitely not. In retrospect she realized that the editor was just a really chatty guy. She should have been putting limits on their conversations and keeping them brief but he just loved to talk. She was so flattered and honored to be involved in this project. She would recommend authors be attuned to this issue because there can be political repercussions which she was not aware of until it was over.

Having learned from that experience, Pat has ever since limited her phone calls with her publishers. She has been self-employed since 1987 and her time is billable. It's even more important for her to keep phone calls brief so that she can be producing income.

Working with Peer Reviewers' Comments

Chapters may be reviewed when they are close to their final form. If you are working with a traditional publisher, they may select blind reviewers. If you are writing a self-published book, you may ask other people with expertise in the subject matter to act as your reviewers. In that case, you will not be getting a blind review. They know the source of the material.

It's much easier to recruit reviewers than it is authors. (Recruitment of authors is discussed in Chapter 13.) The reviewers typically are honored to be asked to be involved. The publisher should list the reviewers in the book, or the editor acknowledges their valuable contributions in the foreword. The reviewers may be listed in the front or back of the book. It's easier to find them in the front of the book, and it gives them more prominence. Some reviewers ask for a free copy of the book. Typically the publisher does not agree. This is a point to negotiate in the contract.

The role of the reviewer is the same whether the book is self-published or being printed by an existing publisher. The reviewers typically read one or more chapters. The reviewer might be selected based on the content of that chapter or asked to go through several chapters.

The reviewer is asked the same kinds of questions as those who review article submissions for journals for a peer-reviewed publication:

- Is this material focused?
- Does it meet the needs of the audience?
- Is it complete?
- What should be eliminated from the material?
- What would you suggest to be added?

- What's your overall impression of this material?

The reviewer is not a copyeditor or a coauthor. This is not always obvious to the reviewer unless the author or editor of the book defines the role. The reviewer might point out typos but is not expected to rewrite the material. It is very important to explain the role to a reviewer, if you are in the process of finding people.

Pat had an experience with a reviewer who misunderstood the role and took it upon herself to edit the chapter, add a lot of new material and then wanted to be named as a co-author of the chapter. The author did not want a co-author and was more than a little offended. She ended up having to take out all the material (which was good material) that would have strengthened the chapter, because the original author was not interested in having a co-author. It was really an unpleasant experience.

When you are the author, do not fall into the trap of thinking your work is perfect and cannot be improved upon. Be willing to listen to the perspective of the reviewer. Sometimes reviewers come up with strange comments that are not appropriate. Authors have the right to reject those comments if they think they are off target but should to listen to what the reviewer says and determine if the project needs to be refocused.

In addition to the reviewers giving you feedback that improves the quality of the book, sometimes they will write the testimonials that will go on a web page or on the back of the book. It's another way of recognizing them, helping them in their career and importantly also helping the status of the book. You want them to provide quotes that are pertinent to the material and are specific quotes, as opposed to "Good chapter", which doesn't tell us anything. A better quote is "This chapter will help you understand the nuances of the HIPAA regulations and it's an essential reading for anyone involved in medical records."

Authors and publishers love testimonials because they are evidence of social proof and can be used in marketing the book. They show that somebody has read the material and approves of it. Testimonials are particularly valuable if the reviewer is a prominent person whose name will be recognized by the audience of the book; it enhances the credibility of the project.

Chapter 13
Copyediting and Page Proof

Chapter 13 Copyediting and Page Proof

This chapter assumes you are the author of a manuscript that will be published by a publisher who uses copyeditors. If you are self-publishing, you may subcontract the job of copyediting, or have someone who is very skilled do it as a favor. You have the option to do the layout of the book (format it with consistent headers) or also subcontract that aspect of the project. Individuals who are skilled in copyediting and layout can be found through elance.com or guru.com.

After the reviewer stage and rewriting stage, you are ready to go through a final checklist. Check to see if your formatting has totally conformed to the publisher's requirements.

- Is your format consistent?
- If you tab over the beginning of each paragraph, like in this book, did you do that consistently throughout?
- Is the font and punctuation in the headers consistent?
- Can you match up each endnote with a reference, or do you have two of the same number, or did you skip numbers? (It is so easy for this to happen.)
- Are your computer files backed up in duplicate?

The material is revised and turned over in as final form as possible following the publisher's guidelines. The publisher is not going to change your references and insert the footnotes. All of that has to be done according to what the publisher wants in terms of the style.

Copyeditors come into the project at the end when the manuscript is final. Traditional publishers employ them and self-publishers will also obtain benefit from having a copyeditor involved in the project. Another person can often catch changes that need to be made that you as the author might not see.

The copyeditor's job is to:

- edit the work to improve word flow,
- correct grammatical or spelling errors,
- find discrepancies in references,
- create a list of questions to ask the author (called "queries"),
- verify the author has turned over all of the needed permission forms to reprint material from another source, and
- layout the manuscript into chapters and insert figures and tables into the chapter.

In the past, copyeditors used double spaced printed copies of the manuscript, handwrote changes in different color pens, and mailed the pages to the authors for review and to answer the queries. This stage is called "copyediting". Now this may be done on pages that are laid out like a finished product.

Sometimes the copyeditor unintentionally changes the meaning of a sentence by editing it. The author should always check every change by a copyeditor to be sure the alteration adheres to the original meaning of the material. The author may note "stet" by a sentence that has been unacceptably altered by the copyeditor. The word "stet" means please restore the sentence to the way it was originally written.

Review the copyedited work very carefully, sentence by sentence. It's a long process to go through and read every chapter to see how it's been edited. You have to make sure that it makes sense, to make sure that you can accept the changes. By now, since you have written all the words in the book, you have read and re-read them in an editing process, read and re-read them in light of the reviewers' comments. Then you get your copyedited chapters and you have to read them sentence by sentence. You may even feel, "I can't look at this thing anymore, I can't stand to read that sentence one more time." The way to counter this is to try to avoid doing too much proofreading at one sitting. You have to push through that stage to get it done.

Recall the advice to pick a topic you really love. This is one of the reasons you have picked something that you really, really, really love because you are going to be living with it for so long. When you are reading and re-reading and thinking about it for so long, it better be a topic you like a lot.

In the second stage, the publisher's staff inputs the changes you have made on the manuscript pages.

The chapters laid out the way they are to appear in the book. This is the "page proof stage". The author sees the material again and approves the page proof. If you are self-publishing the book, you will be involved in this stage.

Make sure that the figures are laid out the way they are supposed to. In other words, figure 7 should not appear three pages before it's mentioned in the text, for example. Or that you don't have long gaps in the text such as the middle of a sentence on one page and then five pages later, after the figures have been inserted, then the rest of the sentence appears. That's very awkward and needs to be fixed.

After the author reviews the changes and answers queries, the copyeditor makes the changes. Typically, the author sees the manuscript one more time, with an opportunity to make limited changes. This is not the time to rewrite chapters. Some publishers have penalty clauses that cost the author money for making too many changes at the page proof stage.

Depending on the traditional publisher, you may have some opportunity to offer thoughts on colors for the cover. When you have had some input in terms of the design of the book and the color of the background, then it becomes even more your creation. Of course, when you self-publish, you have control over the look of the covers. Look at the colors of the covers of other books published about your general topic and emulate them.

Once the manuscript has gone back and forth a couple of times, then the book goes off to the printer and that's the last that you see of it until it comes back to you from the printer. It is always exciting when you get your physical copy of the book in hand. Many people enjoy the smell of a new book and the fact this was *their* new book. It is an emotional experience, a wonderful experience.

Chapter 14
Secrets of Contributed Books

Chapter 14 Secrets of Contributed Books

Formats

A contributed book results when you as the editor recruit people to be contributors to the book. These authors will write a chapter or chapters for the book. This is different than if you write the book entirely yourself or if you and a co-author write the book. The chapters could be written by a small core of people or every chapter could be written by a different person.

Another form of a contributed book that is prevalent in some segments of the writing population is to couple a book to bonuses. A book launch may involve soliciting bonus offers from authors or those unrelated to writing the book. A bonus offer might consist of a free ebook, a free consultation, or other services. Typically there are 20 or 30 of these offers. The person who offers the bonus gains exposure and the possibility of income from a steady client.

A self-published book may be put together by a different author for each chapter, under the direction of an editor. One or more of the chapters may be written by a famous name, whose fame is supposed to encourage book sales. Commonly, the authors are asked to commit to purchase a specific number of copies of each book. The editor uses this strategy to reduce the financial risks.

Picking a Topic

Market research should precede a decision to create a contributed book. These can be enormous undertakings. Pat has been the editor or coeditor of several contributed books. The largest had 54 chapters and four editors. She was the chief editor of another 50-chapter book, and the editor or coeditor of six smaller books, many of which have been revised for new editions.

It is essential to look at a topic for a book and ask yourself if you know enough about this topic to put together the chapters. When you recognize that you want to cover a topic in a broad manner, then you may realize that you need to have contributors who have particular expertise.

The Roles of the Editor Organizer

The editor is the person who is organizing this whole effort. You develop the list of chapters. As the editor, you are recruiting different people to come in and write chapters for you. This is even more relationship oriented than writing a book as a single author or even with a co-author. You set the deadlines for drafts. The publisher gives the editors of the book a deadline for turning over the manuscript, but the editor sets up the interim deadlines, which may go in a contract sent to the contributors.

In one book which Pat edited, the deadline had to be extended for six months because one author didn't turn in material, had two chapters and was months past the deadline. The publisher and Pat chose to wait for the material rather than to replace it because the material was integral to the book. But it was very concerning to everybody when the book got so thrown off of schedule because of one person.

Editor as Project Manager

Writing a book is a project. Often as editor, you are responsible for enforcing deadlines, keeping a schedule, and making sure that the overall publication is completed on time and with the desired quality. Meeting just one of these goals is hard. Meeting both is often challenging.

You can maximize your chances of creating a great book by setting your goals explicitly at the start of a project:

- What is your target publication date?
- How much working time or money do you plan to spend?
- What will your final book look like?
- What quality measures are you aiming for?

"Quality measures" may include a wide variety of goals, including quantitative goals like Flesch Kincaid reading level scores. Often you will have qualitative goals for your book as well, like "easy to read" or "be the 'Bible' for my industry." Knowing these goals at the start of your book project will not guarantee success, but it will at least give you the opportunity to review them regularly and to measure your progress towards success.

Once you have goals for your book, you can start to think about creating a schedule for the work involved in creating, publishing, and marketing the book. Some authors and editors use software like Microsoft Project to manage their deadlines, schedules, and budgets. It is often easier to create your plan simply as a list of milestones, and to manage it using your favorite "to do list" or calendaring software. No matter what tools you use to manage your schedule, creating a plan will help you stay on track. Particularly if your project includes multiple contributors, having a schedule is critical to making sure that the book is actually going to be published.

One of the most valuable contributions of a traditional book publisher to a book writing project is something that they usually require in the initial proposal – deadlines for writing and publishing the book. If you are self-publishing, it is even more important for you to set a deadline for yourself. Too many books are left partly written and unpublished because the author was unable to actually finish the work. It can be hard to finally say that the work is "good enough" to publish. Having a deadline will help give you the discipline to actually get
the book edited and printed.

Recruiter

Finding chapter authors can be difficult. People who have the expertise to write are often very busy. If you are working with a traditional publisher, sometimes the publisher will have suggestions for authors. He may know an author who did a book on that topic. Maybe that person will be able to write a chapter for you. Sometimes, your authors know somebody who would be a good author for another chapter. Most of the time the editor approaches individuals and asks them if they would do a chapter.

When you recruit authors, explain:
- Scope of the project
- Expected length of the chapter
- Deadlines
- Benefits of being published
- The opportunity to coauthor the chapter
- Compensation, if any

One of the questions that comes up is compensation for authors. Some authors enjoy writing, see the benefits to their career, and will willingly contribute without compensation. Others ask, "Are you going to give me royalties?" If the answer is "no," they may lose interest.

One of the difficulties with giving royalties to authors of contributed books is that there is usually very little money to distribute. If you have a book with 45 chapters and you gave people a percentage of the royalties, they might get a check twice a year for a few dollars. This may create resentment. If you provide people a check that small, it's like an insult to them. It's better to offer them a free copy of the book and not try to parse down the money to that finite level. There are some individuals who say, "If I don't get paid for this, I am doing it." Say to yourself, "Okay, next." Find somebody else who will want to be involved in the project and see the benefits to being a published author or having a chapter in the book. Sometimes there is a lot of time spent on the recruitment stage.

Typically the authors get a free copy of the book, whatever is negotiated.

Editor as Educator
Theoretically, when you have more people involved in the job, the process of creating the book should take less time. In reality, a contributed book, particularly one with more than 12 chapters, involves a lot of work. First, the authors are recruited. They should be asked to sign an Author Information Form that will help you, the editor, keep in touch with them. The form also defines the deadlines and asks the author to commit, in writing, to meeting the deadline. See **Figure 1.**

Once the project is underway, the role of the editor shifts from recruiter to educator. The educator role comes into play when working with the authors. Each author needs to receive clear direction on the audience, the focus, and the format for the chapter. **Appendix C** provides an example of guidelines Pat and her coeditor, Barbara Levin, developed to provide to authors of a contributed book. They were accompanied by the publisher's specific formatting guidelines.

The Editor as Author
If you have, as an editor, agreed to write some of the chapters of the book, which Pat has done in all of her books, you have not only your own chapters to

write but also the contributors to work with and the initial editing of their material. The temptation is great to agree to write a lot of chapters in this book that you are editing because you, naturally, have picked a topic that you are passionate about, that you care about deeply. The temptation is great to say, "I can author six of these chapters but I just need five other people to do the other five."

Do not do what Pat has done in the past which is to sign on for too many chapters. Keep your own chapters to an absolute minimum and put your concentration on working with the authors. It will be a smoother process if you do it that way.

Editor as Copyeditor

By now you can see that the editor wears many hats. Some of the authors you recruit will be skilled writers; others will need help with grammar, word flow, and punctuation. Your job is to make sure they've adhered to the formatting guidelines. You will also check the references to be sure that each citation is listed at the end of the chapter. Some authors think you will rewrite their material. Editors typically do not do this. Clarify your role and expectations for the quality of their material.

Figure 1 Author Information Form
Please complete, sign, and fax or email to your primary editor by x/x/xx

Name:

Name of Chapter:

Work Address:

Work Phone Number:

Hours we may contact you at work:

Home Address:

Home Phone Number:

Hours we may contact you at home:

E-mail address:

I agree to the following:

I agree to send a letter with the outline by xx/xx/xx. I agree to submit the first draft by xx/xx/xx and the final draft by xx/xx/xx.

Signature
Date

Your primary editor is__ ____ Please use the contact information to reach your primary editor. If you cannot reach this person, contact the other editor.

Your Name
Your coeditor's name

Chapter 15
Tips for Working with a Coeditor of a Contributed Book

Chapter 15 Tips for Working with a Coeditor of a Contributed Book

Once your plan for your book includes 12 chapters or so, you will usually need help from a coeditor. All of the criteria for picking a coauthor apply to picking a coeditor, and then some. A coeditor needs to be detail-oriented, good at managing people, diligent, and easy to work with. The typical role of the coeditors involves splitting the responsibility for chapters up between them, recruiting authors, and keeping the authors on track. The editors answer questions, review outlines and drafts, and serve as cheerleaders to keep the authors enthused about their chapter and its contribution to the book. The editors may find it valuable to keep tables, such as the one in **Figure 2,** which gives an overview of the chapters and author names.

You should have good communication with your coeditors. Set up regular conference calls and discuss issues that are arising. These most frequently have to do with recruiting authors, adherence to deadlines, as well as work product that is not of acceptable quality. Chapter 14 discusses these issues in more depth.

Coeditors can have life events that make it difficult, if not impossible to participate in a project. This requires re-examination of the work yet to be done and how the slack can be picked up. One of Pat's coeditor's parents died during work on a contributed book. Pat took over the entire project until the coeditor was able to resume her role.

Chief Editor with Associate Editors

In this model, the chief editor recruits associate editors. The associate editors recruit the authors. The chief editor works with the associate editors to keep the project on schedule. When Pat served as the editor the first time for a book for the American Association of Legal Nurse Consultants, she spent about 20 hours a week of uncompensated time for about six months. She recruited and guided eight associated editors. She was not writing the 45 chapters – she was working with her associate editors who were working with their five or six or seven authors.

Pat also edited all of the chapters. She had to fill in for two associate editors who could not complete their responsibilities. She also wrote or coauthored 3 chapters. That gives you the sense of a time commitment for a project of this nature. Pat ran her business in the rest of the hours of the week. While this was a huge commitment, it established Pat's name within the legal nurse consulting industry. People tell her, "You wrote The Bible of our field."

This type of commitment may not be representative of your project, but it gives you an idea of the hours involved in writing. If you enjoy the process they tend to go by pretty quickly. If you don't like the process then, you have to figure out if it's something that you want to do. Or figure out another way to get it accomplished, such as hiring a ghostwriter or freelancer. Remember that your name is going to go on the project and you want the quality to fairly represent you.

Figure 2 Chapter Listing

Name of book or volume of book if more than one	
Title of chapter	Author(s)

The table may be modified to add additional columns, such as one that updates the editor on the status of the work (**Figure 3**). The more authors (and coauthors of each chapter) involved, the more follow up the editors need to do.

Figure 3: Table for keeping track of chapters in a multi-chapter, multi-editor book

		Volume 1: Foundations of Nursing Practice	Status
Editor			
Iyer	1	Roots of Patient Injury Pat Iyer	12/11 Pat is revising this.

Powell	2	Inside Look at Today's Healthcare Environment Judy Rottkamp	12/13 Author is revising
Ashton	44	Nurse Practitioner Pat Goode	12/10 Author is working on this, projects to be done 4/16
Levin	50	Wounds Martie Hawkins	12/14 She is revising

Chapter 16
Working with Authors

Chapter 16 Working with Authors

The most frequent challenges editors face are these:

- helping authors adhere to deadlines
- dealing with work product that is not of acceptable quality
- recruiting replacement authors

Deadlines

Your job as editor is to determine a reasonable deadline for completing your book. The timing may be based on a large national conference, where sales are expected to be high. Your book may need to be released at a certain time because of a seasonal event. Whatever the factors that drive the completion date, it is your job as editor to keep people on target with the deadlines. Easier said than done.

One of the challenges in working with authors is to have people adhere to deadlines. So while it seems like it might be faster to produce a book of contributed chapters than writing the whole thing alone, life events get in the way. The realities are that in any project there will be at least one, and hopefully not more, person who will agree to write a chapter and something will come up – an illness, a marriage, a divorce, a fracture, a lightning strike that destroys a computer, you name it. All kinds of things can happen that will throw that person's life into turmoil and derail the writing plans.

It is difficult for an editor to have an individual who promises and promises and promises to turn the material over and then doesn't meet those deadlines. While it seems clear to say, "Then you just have to cut him off", there is a tendency for an inexperienced editor to believe all those promises and want to give that individual every benefit of the doubt. What happens then is that it becomes too late to replace that person and then the book has to be published without that piece.

The most desirable way to handle these issues is to be very clear on deadlines, to ask the author to sign an agreement that the deadlines will be adhered to.

Unusable material
Another difficult point occurs when the chapter is turned in and is unusable. Carefully review the first draft. If it is not of acceptable quality, have a frank discussion with the author about the level of quality that is expected. A few authors have expected the editor to rewrite their inadequate material. Resist the urge and place the problem back on the author. Attempt to avoid this problem by providing authors with a sample chapter so they can see the expected format and length of the material. Some editors ask authors for a writing sample of a published article, for example.

It is important to be firm, as the editor, when you see trouble signs – material late, off target, or of poor quality. If at all possible, pick people who have a reputation of having written before. You don't want a chapter to be first thing that that individual has ever written in his or her life.

Pat recalls receiving a chapter that was pieced together by 6 coauthors. No one took the role of making it mesh, and it was too disjointed to use. She has rejected other chapters because they were too short and the author was not willing to expand the material. If it is late and unusable, you may have to do without that chapter.

Recruitment after the project is underway
Whenever possible attempt to recruit a replacement author for a chapter that is missing because the author has not adhered to deadlines or submitted unacceptable material. It's often difficult for the replacement author to come in and pick up speed quickly. It puts that person at a disadvantage because you are now already into the first draft stage and there is even less time.

Chapter 17
Revision of a Book
for a New Edition

Chapter 17 Revision of a Book for a New Edition

A successful book may be revised into new editions many times. The original authors may move on, with new editors taking over a book. It can live through several decades. While it used to be common for a book to be revised every 5 years, it is now more common to bring out new editions at a faster pace. Readers have higher expectations for updated and current material. By the time a large book is published, the material is already a year or two years old. The perception is we have to bring out a new edition that much sooner. You have to make sufficient changes in the book to be able to say this is new material and it is justifiably a new edition.

Figure 4 displays the process of confirming that the chapter's authors will agree to update their material. If they do not, a new person must be recruited. This was developed when we updated the third edition of *Nursing Malpractice*.

Figure 5 provides examples of scripts to use when approaching people to write or revise a chapter.

Figure 4: Flow Chart for Recruitment

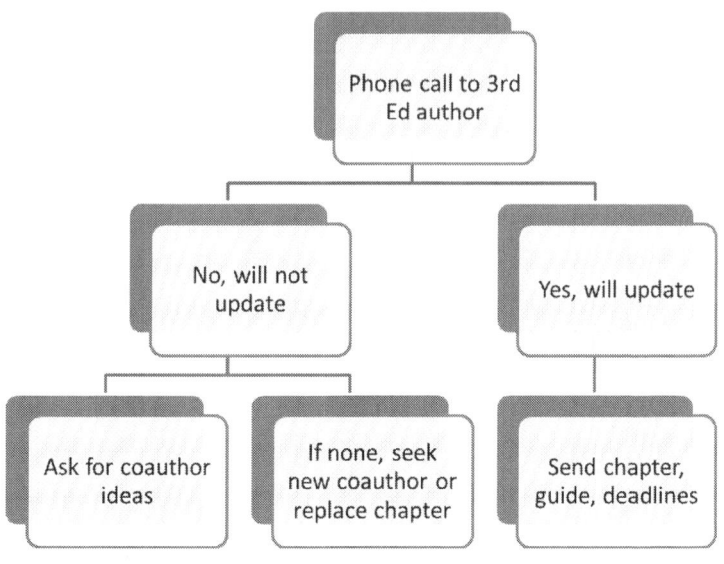

Figure 5: Sample script for how to approach authors

Approaching previous authors and new authors: Sample scripts

Previous author
Hello, I am calling about a chapter you wrote for the third edition of Nursing Malpractice. This text was edited by Pat Iyer and Barbara Levin. It has done well since its original publication in 1996 and has sold out of hardcover books. The publisher has asked us to create a new edition for publication next year. I am working with Pat and Barbara to invite you to participate in the fourth edition by updating your chapter.

Pause – at this point, the author will likely either express interest, ask "What are the deadlines" or say "I'm too busy."

Yes? Great! These are the deadlines: We'll send you the chapter and ask you to modify that for a first draft that is due February 1. The second draft will be due April 1. I'll be your editor. I'll email you the form with the deadlines so you can update your contact information. How does that sound?

It is vital that you return the form within 1 week. What email address should I use to send the chapter, guidelines and deadlines form?

No, you don't want to be involved? We'd appreciate your thoughts about a coauthor to update your chapter. Who can you recommend? Your name will be on the chapter but would be moved to last place.

Approaching new people to coauthor
Hello, I am calling about a text called Nursing Malpractice. I got your name from ***. This text has done well since its original publication in 1996 and has sold out of hardcover books. The publisher has asked us to create a new edition for publication next year. The original author of one of the chapters is unable to update the material and suggested I call you to see if you'd like to have the honor of being published in this book by updating the chapter.

Yes? Great! These are the deadlines: We'll send you the chapter and ask you to modify that for a first draft that is due February 1. The second draft will be due April 1. I'll be your editor. I'll email you the form with the deadlines so you can update your contact information. How does that sound?

It is vital that you return the form within 1 week. I'll send you the chapter, guidelines and deadlines form.

We'll send you a link so you can complete your contract online with the publisher.

If the prospect asks: The authors are not paid royalties because with 50 some chapters in the book, the royalty check would be too small to split. Many of our authors have found that being published in this text opens doors for other opportunities.

No? Who can you recommend?
(Replacing the chapter with a new one is a last resort and done only if original author will not allow a person to add to the chapter.)

New author for new chapter
Hello, I am calling about a chapter for the fourth edition of Nursing Malpractice. This text was edited by Pat Iyer and Barbara Levin. It has done well since its original publication in 1996 and has sold out of hardcover books. The publisher has asked us to create a new edition for publication next year. I got your name from ***. I'd like to include a chapter on ** subject and believe you'd be a great addition to our effort. Would you like to have the honor of being published in this book by adding this chapter? (You may coauthor it if you like.)

Yes? Great! These are the deadlines: I need an outline by January 31st, a first draft by March 1st and a second draft by May 1st. I'll email you the form with the deadlines so you can provide your contact information. How does that sound?

It is vital that you return the form within 1 week. I'll send a sample chapter, author guidelines, and a link so you can complete your contract online with the publisher.

If the prospect asks: The authors are not paid royalties because with 50 some chapters in the book, the royalty check would be too small to split. Many of our authors have found that being published in this text opens doors for other opportunities.

No? Who can you recommend?

Each author should receive guidelines for preparing the manuscript, and the process of setting deadlines begins again.

Updating the material involves these steps:
- Revise the introduction. A study showed that if you change the introduction of a chapter, even if the majority of the material remains the same, the reader views the chapter as new.
- Update the content with new material based on trends or changes applicable to your area.
- Whenever possible, replace older references (over five years) with current sources of information. Add new "additional reading" sources and delete old sources.
- Add new figures if possible. The use of figures and tables breaks up the text and pleases the eye. Remember to renumber the figures if you insert new ones.
- If needed, obtain permission again for the use of figures or tables.

Chapter 18
Copyright

Chapter 18 Copyright

Copyright comes up in several contexts in publishing.

1. Permission to use figures or tables
2. Transfer of copyright to the publisher
3. Use of your material after publication

Permission

The publisher is responsible for providing the editor with information about when and how to obtain permission to use material from another source. Usually, when material is set up as a figure or table in another publication, your author is expected to obtain permission to produce the material in your book. The publisher usually creates a form to use that gives permission to use a specific piece of information in this and subsequent editions of the book. There are exceptions to the need to obtain permission, such as information in the "public domain". This is a subject best discussed with the publisher.

If you are the publisher, do searches online for forms to use to obtain permission for reproduction of content, or speak to an intellectual property attorney to get guidance on the laws.

It can sometimes take months to track down permission; do not leave this for the end. The book cannot go to the printers until all permissions are obtained.

The Publisher's Copyright

When you create a self-published book, you own the copyright. Just the act of putting together the book is one level of copyrighting. When you put copyright and the year on it, that's the second level of copyrighting, and when you register the book with the copyright office. You fill out the paperwork and send in the form and the check. That's another third level of copyrighting. Many authors don't go through that final step of copyrighting of the product with the government but put copyright notice on the material itself. In most cases, that's sufficient protection. Although it is rare to have someone take material you wrote and claim it as their own, copyrighting is there to protect you.

If you write a short article that's going to be published by a journal, typically you are asked to turn over your copyright to the journal so that it can publish the material. There is usually no negotiation on that, just as there is usually no negotiation when you are working with a conventional book publisher who then owns the copyright.

On the other hand, you may recruit an author who does not want to lose copyright. If the publisher will not negotiate, the chapter cannot go into the book. Pat has been involved in three instances of an author refusing to surrender copyright, and this resulted in loss of the chapters. In one instance, she recruited an author who did not want to turn over her copyright to the publisher. The chapter she would have written was expanded to six. Pat edited and self-published the book.

You might, as the author, be able to negotiate the ability to publish the first chapter on your website, as a promotional method to get people to buy the book. These ideas are good to discuss in the beginning when you first see the contract.

Use of the Material After Publication
Turning over the copyright means, you can't take the book and put it on your website verbatim or you can't use the book or portions of it as hand-outs when you are teaching a program. That would be a violation of the copyright law. The material has to be substantially changed, so that it is now new material and then you can use it. In a contributed book, it's important for the authors to know that they can't do that either. They may ask the editor, "I'd like to take my chapter and put it on my website. Or I am teaching a program, and I would like to use the chapter as handouts. May I do that?" The publisher might agree, but say, "Yes, you can but you have to pay by the word to the Copyright Center."

This information may be different in your area or in your industry. Consult with a lawyer for the most up to date information for your particular situation. A lot of these terms of the copyright, whether you are working with a journal or a conventional publisher, are negotiable. Sometimes an author will ask for specific rights which they put in the contract.

Retention of copyright is one of those big advantages when you go self-publishing route. You control all the aspects of self-publishing: all the work you have to put in to actually produce the book, and sometimes the money you have to pay. But on the other hand, you are keeping more control of the book; you don't have to give up so many of those rights.

It is also possible to gain control of the copyright of a book you have previously published with a traditional publisher. If the publisher decides to not bring out a new edition, you may secure the rights, update and distribute the book. There might be a nominal fee or a large fee to gain your own copyright from the publisher, so be sure to ask questions about the process if it is not clear. Pat bought the copyright for her Nursing Documentation book after the third edition and revised it for a fourth edition.

Chapter 19
Publishing Now and in the Future

Chapter 19 Publishing Now and in the Future

Newspapers are fighting for survival. The Internet has resulted in news being available 24-hours a day. News breaks on Twitter faster than it breaks on a website and by the time a newspaper gets the story, it may be "old" news. Newspapers and journals have moved more of their content on line. Some are now totally online.

Similarly, traditional book publishers are having a tougher time. Ebooks and self-publishing have cut into the territory of the traditional publishers. Publishers have merged, changed their willingness to take risks on authors, and now ask for the author's greater involvement in promoting a book.

It's far easier to self-publish now than it ever was before. Anyone with a website can put up any kind of information, about any topic. There are individuals with expertise who can reach markets through blogs and ezines that they could never reach in the traditional format. They can instantly communicate with a following of people who are interested in what they have to say.

There are no grammar police of the Internet. You can see some particularly bad writing with lots of typos and bad grammar. You can write fluently and well and also put it on the Internet at the same time.

If you are an entrepreneurial type as many of us are, then it's far better to be writing today than it was 20 years ago because there is so many different vehicles. Imagine telling somebody 20 years ago, "Would you like that as an MP3 file or a CD? Or would you like to listen to my podcast?" You can communicate with people now in a way that was never possible before. You can communicate with them quickly. There can be something happening today that is in the hands of your interested audience in the form of an article tomorrow and you can't do that in the traditional publishing world.

The prestige of being an author remains. People will pay for content that is pertinent and it's valuable for their needs.

We encourage you to fulfill your ambitions to write. The rewards that it can yield are high. Your life can change in ways you can't foresee, and the satisfaction can be intense.

Appendix A
Improving Your Writing Skills

Appendix A Improving Your Writing Skills

Chapter 1: Grammar Skills

Grammar is a piano I play by ear, since I seem to have been out of school the year the rules were mentioned. All I know about grammar is its infinite power. To shift the structure of a sentence alters the meaning of that sentence, as definitely and inflexibly as the position of a camera alters the meaning of the object photographed. Joan Didion

The answers to the questions are at the end of this appendix on page 191.

Abbreviations
By convention, most abbreviations still require periods. In addition to a.m. and p.m., add periods to i.e., Mr., pp., and e.g.

Spell out an abbreviation the first time it is used. Thereafter, use the abbreviation without defining it.

Use the same abbreviation for both singular and plural units of measurement.

Which is correct?

> Version 1: *The nurse used 1 lb and 6 lb weights.*
>
> Version 2: *The nurse used 1 lb and 6 lbs weights.*

Adverbs
Place an adverb as close as possible to the word it modifies. This applies to "only", "almost", "nearly", "merely" and "also".

Which is correct?

> Version 1: *The sales representative only saw on five clients.*
>
> Version 2: *The sales representative saw only five clients.*

Would you move "only" in the following sentence?

> *A medication found at the hospital bedside can only be deemed contraband if it is used without the permission of the prescriber.*

"Only" usually belongs as close as possible to what it limits. Here, the writer stated, but does not mean, that the medication can be deemed contraband and nothing else. The writer means the medication is defined as contraband only under specified conditions.

The new sentence:

Capitalization
Capitalize proper names. Do not capitalize medical terms.

> *She had hypertension, diabetes, and coronary artery disease.*

Just because these conditions can be abbreviated as HTN, DM, and CAD does not mean they are capitalized when spelled out.

Capitalize the first letter of the first word of sentences, quotations, and listed items (either phrases or sentences).

> *He said, "Why me?"*

Contractions
Contractions establish a personal, informal tone. Avoid their use in a formal report.

> Version 1: *It's my opinion that he didn't understand how to respond to the changing marketplace.*

> Corrected Version 2: *It is my opinion that he did not understand how to respond to the changing marketplace.*

Dangling Modifiers
Dangling modifiers can be adjectives, adverbs, or prepositional phrases. Ensure that modifiers, particularly those expressing action, have a clear noun to modify. Ensure modifiers appear either next to or as close as possible to the word or words modified.

Which are correct?

> Version 1: *Having analyzed the sequence of events, the recommendation was to repeat the clinical trial.*

Version 2: *I analyzed the sequence of events; I recommended we repeat the clinical trial.*

Version 3: *Having analyzed the sequence of events, I recommended we repeat the clinical trial.*

^^^^^^^^^^^^^^^^^^^^^^^^^^^^^^

<u>The best misplaced and dangling modifiers of all time</u> [1]

Oozing slowly across the floor, Marvin watched the salad dressing.

Waiting for the Moonpie, the candy machine began to hum loudly.

Coming out of the market, the bananas fell on the pavement.

She handed out brownies to the children stored in Tupperware.

I smelled the oysters coming down the stairs for dinner.

I brushed my teeth after eating with Crest Toothpaste.

Grocery shopping at Big Star, the lettuce was fresh.

Driving like a maniac, the deer was hit and killed.

With his tail held high, my father led his prize poodle around the arena.

I saw the dead dog driving down the interstate.

Holding a bag of groceries, the roach flew out of the cabinet.

Emitting thick black smoke from the midsection, I realized something was wrong.

The girl was consoled by the nurse who had just taken an overdose of sleeping pills.

I saw an accident walking down the street.

Drinking beer at a bar, the car would not start.

Playing pool in the living room, the radio was turned on by Jim.

Frustrated by diagonal movement, the set was turned off.

Mrs. Daniel sews evening gowns just for special customers with sequins stitched on them.

Although exhausted and weary, the coach kept yelling, "Another lap!"

She carefully studied the Picasso hanging in the art gallery with her friend.

Having an automatic stick shift, Nancy bought the car.

Freshly painted, Jim left the room to dry.

He held the umbrella over Janet's head that he got from Delta Airlines.

He wore a straw hat on his head, which was obviously too small.

After drinking too much, the toilet kept moving.

∧∧∧∧∧∧∧∧∧∧∧∧∧∧∧∧∧∧∧∧∧∧∧∧∧∧∧∧∧

Double negatives
Double negatives make the reader work harder and slow comprehension.

Which is correct?

> Version 1: *It is common for the Human Resources Department to perform reference checks.*
>
> Version 2: *It is not uncommon for the Human Resources Department to perform reference checks.*

Parallel construction
Achieve predictability with parallel construction. For example, this sentence uses three adjectives to describe the subject:

> *The manager was intelligent, charismatic, and persuasive.*

Compare that sentence with this one:

> *The manager was intelligent, charismatic, and she was persuasive.*

Parallel construction can also be achieved by repeating grammatical elements in the same order. This sentence fails to do so:

> *Bullying in the workplace has become more evident - either by employees verbally or nonverbally by supervisors.*

Meet the reader's expectations by reversing the order of the words:

> *Bullying in the workplace has become more evident - either by employees verbally or supervisors nonverbally.*

Reversing the clauses
Have the subject of the sentence as close as possible to the beginning. Do not reverse the clauses.

Which is correct?

> Version 1: *Throughout the trial, the patient had no side effects.*

> Version 2: *The patient had no side effects throughout the trial.*

Run On Sentences
A sentence that fills a paragraph is a run on sentence. You have written a run on sentence if you have to stop several times to breathe when reading the sentence aloud. Break the sentence into other sentences to make it easier for your reader.

Example of a Run On Sentence
American Airlines has worked with many people who are passionate advocates in their community. One such individual is Pat Porter, the longtime head of North Texas Business for Culture and the Arts (NTBCA), a

nonprofit arts-advocacy organization that connects North Texas companies with local agencies and artists to showcase their art improve the community's quality of life, and foster economic development. Porter recently retired from NTBCA after more than 20 years; during that time, she worked closely with American and its Arts Leadership Council, which seeks to affect American's Support of the arts community and to encourage the artistic talents of AA employees, primarily through the annual On My Own Time art show.

Sic

Sic comes from the Latin *sicut*, which means "just as". It is used when you are quoting something that you know was incorrectly stated by the writer.

> *"He wrote, 'The patient had a spinal chord [sic] injury.'"*

Subject and Verb Agreement

Subjects of sentences must agree in number with their verbs. There must be gender agreement between the pronouns and the people to whom they refer.

When "or" or "nor" comes between two subjects, the verb's form agrees with the subject closer to it. [2]

> *He said development of one brochure or several marketing materials was the goal of the campaign.*

Singular subjects take singular verbs, even when a plural phrase comes between them. [3]

> *One of the procedures is on the computer.*

Companies and countries are not humans, so "their" does not apply to them.

What is the correct word before marketing?

> *The company has written _____ marketing plan.*

What is the flaw in this sentence below? (The sentence below will not look wrong to some of you, and to others, it will have the effect of chalk on a blackboard.)

> *An employer is liable for continuing to employ a pharmacist after learning that they have a history of drug abuse.*

This sentence above mixes singular and plural. The "pharmacist" is singular and the pronoun "they" is plural.

Rewrite:

"There's" cannot be used with plural subjects. It stands for "there is" and is singular.

> *There's confusion among the cooks in this kitchen.*

> *There are* (not there's) *many sales representatives in need training.*

Wordiness

Effective editing tightens and simplifies your writing. Look for wordiness, convoluted sentences, and other ways you have distracted or confused the reader.

Consider this sentence:

> *There is no valid reason for the sales force ignoring the application of best practices in this situation.*

Rewritten:

Avoid redundant expressions: null and void, part and parcel, each and every, if and when, save and except, and aid and abet. The redundancy just adds extra words and creates a stilted tone.

Chapter 2: Punctuation

Grammatical correctness of the trivial sort – epitomized by correct use of apostrophes – enhances well-being in the same way that correct behavior does in most social settings: lines at the cashier, meetings of a project team, track meets, parties, and funerals. It helps us to obtain respect, a fair hearing in this world.

> Lawrence Weinstein, *Grammar for the Soul*, 2008

Apostrophes

Use an apostrophe-s after a noun to form a possessive. Find the word you are making possessive by turning the two-word phrase around and inserting "of" or "of the" between the words. [4] In the example below, you can recognize the possessive form because you would say be able to say "the skill of the procurement specialist".

> *The procurement specialist's skill was notable.*

If the word is singular, add apostrophe-s. If the word is plural, add s-apostrophe.

1. *The manager's objection was recorded.*
2. *The managers' objections were recorded.*

How do you handle the situation when the noun is long? Although this sentence is grammatically correct, it creates an unwieldy sentence:

> *The Landscaping Research Institute's continuing education courses are offered nationwide.*

Even though the above sentence is correct, it is awkward. A new version of this sentence could be:

Rewritten:

The apostrophe follows the "s" when a possessive word is singular and already ends with an "s". Some writers may add another "s". Both are considered correct, depending on the name involved.

1. Dr. Jones' reputation was solid.
2. Dr. Jones's reputation was solid.

Some words sound strange when they are used in a possessive sense, as in Kansas or Moses. The possessive forms of these names are: Moses' and Kansas'. [5]

Use the possessive form for the last name of a joint partnership:

I called Drs. Wicker and Gunther's office.

It is optional to use an apostrophe to form the plurals of dates and words comprised of capital letters. A small "s" is used for ease in reading. Both are correct:

1. *ABG's or ABGs*
2. *The 2000s or the 2000's*

Use an apostrophe to form the plural of small letters:

a's, b's, c's

Apostrophes are used in contractions, such as isn't for is not, or can't for cannot. Contractions are not typically used in formal writing.

The absence of an apostrophe from a contraction can cause confusion.

Brackets
Brackets are used to enclose parenthetical or explanatory material that occurs within material that is already enclosed within parentheses.

> *We decided to contact the cardiologists. (Actually the staff physicians at the hospital [Chestershire Medical Center] agreed to meet with our sales force.)*

Capitalization
Capitalize sections of the country and world, but not directions.

> *She is from the East Coast.*

Capitalize the first word of a title and all words within a title except for prepositions, conjunctions, and the words "a", "and" and "the".

> *Dr. Mallick, the Director of Medical Affairs, is in charge of credentialing.*

Colon
A colon introduces the part of a sentence that exemplifies, restates, elaborates, undermines, explains, or balances the preceding part. [6] It makes the second thought the most important part of the sentence. The first part of the sentence before the colon is a complete sentence that could stand on its own.

1. *The support staff needed one thing to remain calm: an experienced supervisor.*
2. *This much is clear, Mr. Talley: it is a difficult sell.*
3. *Joseph Montero had one rule when he came into the office: always check the phone slips for messages.*

Use a sentence or portion of a sentence before bulleted or numbered items in a list. End the sentence with a colon.

The patient had the following medical diagnoses:

- *Hypertension*
- *Obesity*
- *Diabetes mellitus*

A period is placed at the end of each item in a list if it could complete a full sentence.

The office manager was responsible for:
- *hiring new employees.*
- *evaluating each employee.*
- *participating on committees.*

Commas

Commas are used to join two complete sentences.

Mr. Gillis was morbidly obese, and he was short of breath.

Commas separate complete thoughts joined by these simple conjunctions: and, but, or, for, nor, so and yet.

> *Susan was going to call the researcher, but a phone call diverted her.*

A comma is used before a quote.

> *Mr. Gillis said, "I use a sleep apnea monitor at home."*

A comma sets off an interjection.

> *Oh, come on.*

Commas are used after a name when a person is being directly addressed.

> *Ron, I think this problem needs to be quickly addressed.*

Commas are used before an afterthought.

> *This illustration is an effective one, is it not?*

Commas are used in lists of items.

> *She gathered reports, medical records, and pads before heading into the room.*

Commas are used to bracket additional information. The information within the commas is called appositives—words that explain what came before.

> *Robert McKinsey, the supervisor, began the meeting.*

Commas precede "which" clauses.

> *The normal procedure required notification of the CEO, which was the director's responsibility.*

Use a comma when tacking on an "ing" clause that modifies rather than identifies something in the first half of the sentence. [7]

> *The physician refused to see the sales representative, stating he was not interested in getting the samples.*

Dash (en and em)
The en dash is as wide as an "n". It is used to create ranges of dates (2005-2008) or page number ranges (pages 212-215). The American system does not place a space around the dash. The British system uses a space on either side of the en dash (pages 212 – 215). Consistently use either system.

Methods of creating dashes vary with the word processor you use. In some systems, an en dash is created by typing a space and one or two hyphens between words.

The em dash (wide as an "m") is used to make the first thought the most important part of the sentence, or to interrupt a sentence for insertion of thoughts related to, but not a part of, the main idea of the sentence.

> *Lipitor had been undergoing clinical trials – all of these were done abroad – for three years before the patients were withdrawn from the trial.*

An em dash is created when you hit the hyphen key twice and do not include a space before the hyphens. Alternatively, look for a symbol for the em dash in the symbol library of the word processor.

Which type of dash is needed?

1. The clinical trials took place from October 2007 ** January 2009.
2. He was surprised** she had been cooperative up to that point.

Ellipsis
Those three little dots after the end of a sentence mean there is more to come . . .

They are also used when one is quoting selectively from a document and omitting sentences. They are typed as space period space period space period space.

Exclamation point
The exclamation point conveys emotion. It is rarely used in reports. There is a risk of overdoing its use. Limit your use of an exclamation point to no more than one at the end of a sentence.

Hyphen
The hyphen is used when spelling out numbers.

> *She was a 32-year-old white female.*

The hyphen clarifies words that would otherwise be ambiguous.

> *The abscess re-formed after it was drained.*

Hyphens are used to separate the components of a compound word (a noun, adjective or verb).

> *Morphine is a high-risk medication.*

Hyphens are also used to separate units of measure, such as month-long.

Italics
Avoid underlining or excessive use of bold for emphasis. Instead, use italics to make a word or words or the title of a publication stand out.

For the Defense is a leading publication.

Numbers
Spell out a number that forms the first word of a sentence, unless the number is a date.

1. *Two thousand employees were due for a raise in February.*
2. *2008 statistics are now available.*

Add a comma to numbers larger than 999.

The cost was $200,000.

Define ages with figures.

1. *He was a 65-year-old who looked older than his stated age.*
2. *Mary Black, age 45, was the last person hired.*

Spell out numbers up to ten, and use numbers thereafter, unless the sentence contains both numbers under and over ten. Then, choose figures for quantities over and under ten when the items in a sentence are similar. Also note that the numbers below are handily organized from the smallest to the largest number of units.

1. *She spoke at three local meetings, four regional conferences, and six annual conferences.*
2. *She spoke at 3 local meetings, 4 regional conferences and 17 national and international association meetings.*

Simplify large numbers.

Version 1: *A total of $52 million has been spent on healthcare reform campaigning.*

This is an awkward version: Version 2: A total of $52,000,000 has been spent on healthcare reform campaigning.

Spell out and hyphenate fractions.

One-quarter of the patients were affected by nausea.

Parentheses

Use parentheses, rather than commas, when all commas might be confusing. [8]

Mr. Wright (the security guard), Mrs. Nolan, and Mr. Patel responded to the request for help in the cafeteria.

Do not capitalize the first word of the material within parentheses, even if the material is a complete sentence, unless the word is a proper noun or the first word of a quoted sentence. [9] Use a parentheses to explain, such as around words that explain an abbreviation.

1. *Please attend the meeting at 10:00 (we will have space) to discuss the new results of the study.*

> 2. *Please attend the meeting at 12:00 (Mr. Chung will be present) to review the new results of the study.*

Place a period or other punctuation mark outside the closing parenthesis.

> *Will you attend the conference (scheduled for 9:00)?*

Periods
A period at the end of the sentence fits within quotation marks.

> *He said, "I am unable to see why we need a new procedure."*

A period is placed outside the parenthesis if the phrase within the parentheses is not a complete sentence.

> *He said, "I am unable to see why we need a new procedure" (referring to the quarterly reports).*

Periods are used after abbreviations and initials, numbers in a list, and numbers and letters in outlines. Use only one period if an abbreviation ends the sentence.

> *He ran out of the law firm at 11:30 a.m.*

Question marks
Do not use question marks for an indirect question or for statements written as questions but intended as courteous remarks.

> Correct? *During our preliminary investigation, we asked whether the patient was allergic?*

Rewritten:

Quotation marks

Single quotation marks are used to indicate a quotation within a quotation.

> *Mr. Kendrick said, "I was told, 'do not continue' when I asked about continuing the study."*

Place periods inside closing quotation marks.

> *He said, "I did not realize the study was double blind."*

Place semicolons and colons outside of closing quotation marks.

> *The company's financial department provided data during the "first quarter campaign"; the medication's chance of success was slim.*

Semicolon

A semicolon joins two sentences when there is no conjunction between the two parts, such as "and", or "but".

> *The package insert was revised; an evaluation was immediately started.*

Items in a series that include commas are separated by semicolons.

> *He has an office in New York, NY; Parsippany, NJ; and Teaneck, NJ.*

A Love Letter

The Power of Punctuation: Which Letter do You Prefer?

Dear Jack,

I want a man who knows what love is all about. You are generous, kind, thoughtful. People who are not like you admit to being useless and inferior. You have ruined me for other men. I yearn for you. I have no feelings whatsoever when we're apart. I can be forever happy- will you let me be yours?

Jill

Dear Jack,

I want a man who knows what love is. All about you are generous, kind, thoughtful people, who are not like you. Admit to being useless and inferior. You have ruined me. For other men I yearn! For you I have no feelings whatsoever. When we're apart I can be forever happy. Will you let me be?

Yours,

Jill [10]

Chapter 3: Easily Confused Words

One cannot say anything simply and clearly unless one first understands it clearly.

Henry Weihofen, Legal Writing Style, Second Edition, 1980

Accept versus Except
"Accept" is a verb that means "to receive". "Except" refers to "the exclusion of".

> *She accepted a position as a summer intern. She could work in any of the company's offices except for the South Jersey office.*

Aid versus Aide
"Aid" is a verb that means "to help" or a noun that refers to coming to the assistance of another. "Aide" is a person.

> *The certified pharmacy aide came to the aid of the pharmacist.*

Advise versus Advice
"Advice" is a noun. "Advise" is a verb.

> *The manager sought the advice of the director about the needs of the employee. The director advised the manager to praise the employee.*

Affect versus Effect
"Affect" is normally a verb and "effect" is a noun.

> *We can affect the negotiations when we examine the effects of communication.*

Is this sentence correct?

> *The effect of the medication was to change the patient's affect.*

All right versus Alright
"All right" is standard spelling. "Alright" is an informal word and is incorrect. Do not use "alright". [11]

And/Or
"And/or" is awkward. Avoid using it.

And versus To
Which is correct?

> Version 1: *I will try and see what I can do.*
>
> Version 2: *I will try to see what I can do.*

Averse versus Adverse

We are averse to things we find distasteful. We are adverse to our adversaries.

Which is correct?

> Version 1: *He was averse to being outranked.*
>
> Version 2: *He was adverse to being outranked.*

Because versus Since
"Because" provides an explanation.

> *Because well-educated people will be reading your report, you have to be careful how it is written.*

"Since" refers to time.

> *Since when did he stop calling our office to check on his results?*

Between versus Among
Use "between" when choosing between two people or objects.

> *Robert Callendar could not choose between a job offer in Boston versus one in Springfield.*

Use "among" when discussing three or more persons or objects.

> *The employees could not agree among themselves which manager they liked the most.*

Can versus May
"Can" refers to capability to do something. "May" refers to permission to do so.

1. *Can I remember the combination of the locker room?*
2. *May I leave the file in your hands?*

Cite versus Site
"Cite" refers to quoting something. It is used in articles, books, and other writing. "Site" refers to a location, such as a website.

> *The expert went to the site of the American Association of Pharmaceutical Researchers to see if she could definitions to cite in a report.*

Classic versus Classical

"Classic" serves as a standard of excellence. It is often used to refer to something singular or special. Think "Classic Coke", or "classic rock", or "It was a classic story of miscommunication." "Classical" means versed in the classics. Most commonly classical refers to a type of music. Do not substitute "classical" when "classic" is the word you want.

> *It is a classic error to mix up two clients with similar last names.*

Council versus Counsel

A "council" is a group of people. As a noun, a "counsel" or counselor is another name for an attorney, or as a verb, refers to giving advice.

1. *The counsel from both sides decided to negotiate.*
2. *The council decided to pass the regulation.*

Criteria versus Data

Which of these sentences is correct?

1. *The criteria for being given hospital privileges are defined in policies.*
2. *The data are revealing.*

Both are correct, as both criteria and data are plural. The singular of criteria is criterion. The singular of data is datum.

Dependent versus Dependant
Fill in the blanks with dependent or dependant.
Whether a minor is a _____ is _____ in part on the child's age.

Discreet versus Discrete
"Discreet" refers to being prudent or tactful. "Discrete" means "separate or individual". [12]

1. *He was discreet about being gay.*
2. *The surgeon removed five discrete specimens from the left breast.*

Each versus Their
"Each" is singular and refers to only one. It is incorrect to say "Each manager will take care of their employees". This should be reworded to:

Rewritten:

E.g. versus i.e.
These are tricky and frequently misused abbreviations. A knowledge of Latin proves useful in distinguishing between the two. Since many of us never had Latin, here is the short cut for figuring out the difference between the two. E.g. means *exempli gratia*. It is used when you want to choose between different examples. It may help to mentally link the "e" in e.g. or exempli gratia" to the "e" in "example".

The director requested to see the marketing material, e.g. photographs and verbiage.

I.e. stands for *id est*, which means "that is". I.e. can be used for "in other words". It may help to mentally link the "i" in i.e. to the "i" in "in other words".

> *The director masterminded the campaign, i.e. she oversaw every detail.*

Should i.e. or e.g. be used here?

Christina asked to see the notes about the employee's performance, ____ the manager's anecdotal reports.

Envelop versus Envelope
"Envelop" means to surround and enclose. "Envelope" is a noun.

> 1. *She wanted to envelop him in an embrace.*
> 2. *Bills are mailed in envelopes.*

Etc.
Etc. is considered an evasion for listing all of the details or facts. Avoid using it in formal writing. If you really need to use the concept, substitute "and so on".

Forward versus Foreword
"Forward" is a direction. "Foreword" is a noun that means the introduction of a book.

> 1. *He headed forward down the hall.*
> 2. *We asked a prominent person to write a foreword for our book.*

Further versus Farther
Farther refers to distance. Further refers to "more".

1. *The patient found the distance to the diabetologist's office was farther than he expected.*
2. *The doctor altered the medical plan to further diagnose the patient's problems.*

Have versus Of
Although we might say, "I woulda, shoulda, coulda done something different", we write more formally in reports created in the business setting. Use "have" after a verb such as "would", "should" and "could".

Correct?

I should of locked the door to the office.

Insure versus Ensure
"Insure" relates to insurance. "Ensure" is to achieve something.
You buy insurance to insure your car, and to ensure peace of mind.

Its and It's
Its is possessive.

The accounts receivable department changed its procedure for collecting money.

It's is a contraction for "it is".

It's a surprise the supplier said that.

Lay, Laid, Lie, and Lain
The verb "lay" means to put or to place. It must have an object.

1. *The grounds maintenance department promised to lay the sod on the front lawn.*
2. *She laid the blame at the feet of the managing partner.*

Lie and lain are the part of the verb "lie", meaning to rest or recline. "Lie" cannot have an object.

1. *The entrance lies south of Route 202.*
2. *That supply of salt has lain there for over a month.*

Loose versus Lose

What is wrong with this sentence?

She had nothing to loose.

To lose is to let go of something. To loosen is to make something slack.

1. Correct: *She had nothing to lose.*
2. Correct: *The nurse loosened the patient's clothing.*
3. Correct: *The patient was losing consciousness.*

Me, Myself and I

This may be everyone's favorite topic but the words are not interchangeably used.

Which is correct?

Version 1: *The manager spoke to my supervisor and me about marketing methods.*

Version 2: *The manager spoke to my supervisor and myself about marketing methods.*

An easy way to figure out when "me" is correct is to take away "my supervisor". You will be able to see or hear the correctness of this sentence: *The managing partner spoke to me about marketing methods.*

Which is correct?

Version 1: *The managing partner spoke to my supervisor and I about marketing methods.*

Version 2: *The managing partner spoke to my supervisor and me about marketing methods.*

Is this correct?

Me and my sister went to the show.

None, Everyone, and Anyone

These words are singular – even "everyone". An easy way to remember this is to recognize that each word has "one" in it.

Everyone sees the need to ensure cash flow. None of them is disputing that. Anyone who sees a way to generate income is responsible to take action.

Personnel versus Personal

"Personnel" are employed by a company. "Personal" refers to something that pertains to you.

Principle versus Principal
It is important to live by principles that govern behavior. Both "principle" and "rule" end in "le". A "principal" is a person who is a head of a school, a notable person in a firm, or a debt. This means "most important".

Fill in the blank

The _____ reason I went to see the _____ of the firm was because I could not accept the _____ of the decision-making process.

Rational versus Rationale
"Rational" is an adjective that means logical, or in medical terms, capable of understanding. "Rationale" is an explanation for something. Nurses take care of lots of patients who are not rational.

A rational person would understand the rationale for the restriction.

What is correct word for the blank?

He agreed with the _____ for the study.

Regardless versus Irregardless
"Regardless" means without regard. "Irregardless" is not a word because you cannot say without regard twice. Using "irregardless" will identify you as lacking skill. Do not use it.

Regime versus Regimen
A totalitarian regime is a dictatorship. A patient undergoes a treatment regimen.

He was tortured under the dictator's regime.
A newly diagnosed diabetic has to master a treatment regimen.

Ruminate versus Marinate
To ruminate means to consider something, to think it over. To marinate means to put a food item in a sauce and let the spices seep into the food.

Stationary versus Stationery
"Stationary" means fixed in one spot. Stationery" is a noun that means paper.
The exercise bike was stationary.
She used stationery to write to the president of the association.

They're, Their and There
"They're" is a contraction for "they are".
They're coming up the walkway.
"Their" refers to the possessive.
It is in their best interest to adhere to the policy.
"There" is a location.
She went over there to work the evening shift.

Then versus Than
"Then" refers to a point in time.
Boris went to the cafeteria, and then got his lunch.
"Than" is used for comparisons.
> *The companion had more job applicants than openings.*

Who's versus Whose
"Who's" is the contraction for "who is". "Whose" is the possessive form of the pronoun "who".[13]

1. *Who's that climbing out the window?*
2. *She was the supervisor whose staff called in sick the most.*

You're versus Your

"You're" is a contraction for "you are".

> *You're going to get in trouble for being absent without notifying the office manager.*

"Your" is possessive.

> *Your company will benefit from the services of a skilled law firm.*

Answers

Bold signifies the correct answer.

Version 1: The nurse used 1 lb and 6 lb weights.
Version 2: The nurse used 1 lb and 6 lbs weights.

Version 1: The sales representative only saw on five clients.
Version 2: The sales representative saw only five clients.

Rewritten sentence:
A medication found at the hospital bedside can be deemed only contraband if it is used without the permission of the prescriber.

Bold is correct:

Version 1: *Having analyzed the sequence of events, the recommendation was to repeat the clinical trial.*

Version 2: *I analyzed the sequence of events; I recommended we repeat the clinical trial.*

Version 3: *Having analyzed the sequence of events, I recommended we repeat the clinical trial.*

Bold is correct:

> ***Version 1: It is common for the Human Resources Department to perform reference checks.***
>
> Version 2: *It is not uncommon for the Human Resources Department to perform reference checks.*

Bold is correct:

> Version 1: Throughout the trial, the patient had no side effects.
>
> **Version 2: The patient had no side effects throughout the trial.**

What is the correct word before marketing?

> The company has written **its** marketing plan.

> An employer is liable for continuing to employ a pharmacist after learning that they have a history of drug abuse.

Rewrite:

> An employer is liable for continuing to employ a pharmacist after learning that the pharmacist has a history of drug abuse.

Rewrite this sentence:

> There is no valid reason for the sales force ignoring the application of best practices in this situation.

Rewritten:

There is no valid reason for the sales force to ignore best practices.

> The Landscaping Research Institute's continuing education courses are offered nationwide.

Rewritten:

The continuing education courses of the Landscaping Research institute are offered nationwide.

Which type of dash is needed?

1. The clinical trials took place from October 2007-January 2009.
2. He was surprised–she had been cooperative up to that point.

Rewrite this sentence:

During our preliminary investigation, we asked whether the patient was allergic?

Rewritten:

We asked whether the patient was allergic during our preliminary investigation.

Is this sentence correct?

The effect of the medication was to change the patient's affect.

Yes, this is correct. Affect is a mood.

Which is correct?

Version 1: *I will try and see what I can do.*

Version 2: *I will try to see what I can do.*

The second sentence is less casual. Similarly, use "try to see" and "try to bring", rather than "try and see" or "try and bring".

Which is correct?

Version 1*: He was averse to being outranked.*

Version 2: *He was adverse to being outranked.*

Fill in the blanks with dependent or dependant.
Whether a minor is a _____ is _____ in part on the child's age.
Whether a minor is a dependant is dependent in part on the child's age.

"Each manager will take care of their employees."

Rewritten:
Each manager will take care of his or her employees.

Should i.e. or e.g. be used here?

Christina asked to see the notes about the employee's performance, ____ the manager's anecdotal reports.

Christina asked to see the notes about the employee's performance, i.e. the manager's performance evaluations.

Correct?

I should of locked the door to the office.

This should be rewritten as

I should have locked the door to the office.

Which is correct?

Version 1: *The manager spoke to my supervisor and me about marketing methods.*

Version 2: *The manager spoke to my supervisor and myself about marketing methods.*

Which is correct?

Version 1: *The managing partner spoke to my supervisor and I about marketing methods.*

Version 2: *The managing partner spoke to my supervisor and me about marketing methods.*

Rewrite this sentence:

Me and my sister went to the show.

Rewritten:

My sister and I went to the show.

Fill in the blank

The _____ reason I went to see the _____ of the firm was because I could not accept the _____ of the decision-making process.

The principal reason I went to see the principal of the firm was because I could not accept the principles of the decision-making process.

Rational or rationale?
He agreed with the _____ for the study.
He agreed with the rationale for the study.

Chapter 4: Proofreading

Proofreading Symbols

Symbol	Meaning	Example
↓	insert a comma	The mayor's brother I tell you is a crook.
⌄	apostrophe or single quotation mark	I wouldnt know where to put this vase.
∧	insert something	I know it in fact, everyone knows it.
⌄⌄	use double quotation marks	May favorite poem is Design.
⊙	use a period here	This is a declarative sentence
⌿	delete	The elephant's trunk is is really its nose.
∼	transpose elements	He only picked the one he likes.
◯	close up this space	Jordan lost his favorite basket ball.
#	a space needed here	I have only threefriends. Ted, Raoul, and Alice.
¶	begin new paragraph	"I know it," I said. "I thought so," she replied.
No ¶	no paragraph	"I knew it, she said. No ¶ "He's no good."
/	lowercase	Lunch was Delicious.
=	capitalize	Tell me what i should do.

Appendix B Resources

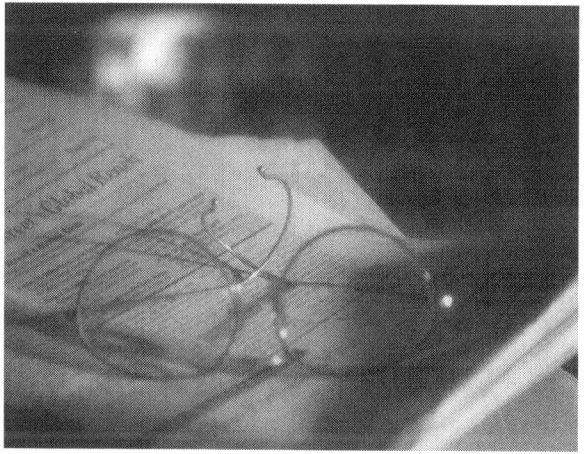

Appendix B Resources

If you are weak in writing, get a good book on grammar or go to the library and take out a book to refresh yourself. Do an Internet search, and you'll find some sites that will help with basic skills.

If you are a professional speaker and qualify for membership in the National Speakers Association, join the group. There are criteria to join the organization that can be found out by going to the website of the National Speakers Association (**www.nsaspeaker.org**). The organization is of tremendous value for those who combine speaking and writing. There is a special interest group for people interested in writing and publishing. If you are a good writer and you enjoy the process and you become an expert on it, then you may develop an interest in speaking. Conversely, you may start as a speaker, and through that expertise, write a book.

This is a partial list of resources that may be of value to you. They are primarily useful for people who want to self-publish. Review their websites and determine if they will meet your needs.

SelfPublishing
51 E. 42nd Street
New York, NY 10017
www.selfpublishing.com
212-616-4206

360 Digital Books
8089 Stadium Drive, Suite C
Kalamazoo, MI 49009
www.360digitalbooks.com
866-379-8767 ext 1

Stylematters
3720 Spruce Street, Suite 426
Philadelphia, PA 19104
www.style-matters.com
866-792-6164

Infinity Publishers Inc
1094 New DelHaven Street, Suite 100
West Conshohocken, PA 19428
www.infinitypublishing.com
610-941-9999

Sheridan Books, Inc.
100 N. Staebler Road
Ann Arbor, MI 48103
www.sheridan.com
800-999-2665

The Book Shepherd
Judith Briles
14160 E. Bellewood Dr.
Aurora, CO 80015
www.TheBookShepherd.com
303-885-2207

Smith Publicity
1930 E. Marlton Pike, Suite 1-46
Cherry Hill, NJ 08003
www.smithpublicity.com
856-489-8654

Worzalla
2378 East Bear Hill Drive
Draper, UT 84020
www.worzalla.com
866-523-7737

Bookbaby
www.bookbaby.com
877-961-6878

Appendix C
Author Guidelines

Appendix C
Author Guidelines

This is a sample of material to send to contributors for a book. It acts as a road map to help the authors achieve success.

Please read through these instructions and refer to them again before sending us any material.

1. The Editors
(describe the editors)
Example:

Pat Iyer MSN RN LNCC has coauthored or edited 25 books since 1986 including Nursing Home Litigation, Investigation and Case Preparation, Medical Legal Aspects of Pain and Suffering, Medical Legal Aspects of Medical Records, Nursing Malpractice, Nursing Documentation: A Nursing Process Approach, among others. She was the sole editor of the all three editions of Nursing Malpractice, and the chief editor of Legal Nurse Consulting Principles and Practices, and Business Principles of Legal Nurse Consulting, both produced for the American Association of Legal Nurse Consultants (AALNC). Pat is an experienced legal nurse consultant. She served as president of AALNC.

Barbara Levin BSN, RN, CMSRN, ONC, LNCC has served as an associate editor of the Legal Nurse Consulting Principles and Practices, and Medical Legal Aspects of Medical Records and Nursing Malpractice,

Third Edition. This is her third collaboration with Pat. She testifies as an orthopaedic nursing expert witness and served as president of AALNC.

One of the two of us will be identified to you as your primary editor.

2. Deadlines
The preparation of this manuscript is on a fast track. We strongly recommend that you pace yourself and avoid waiting until close to the deadline to complete the project. Our plan is as follows:
Outline due: March 20, 2012
First draft due: June 1, 2012
Final draft due: September 1, 2012
Publication: Mid-year 2013

3. Failure to Meet the Deadlines
If you are unable to meet any deadline, please advise us immediately. We have the ability to give you a week or two leeway, but we are unable to provide more flexibility than that. We selected you to update or add a chapter because of our confidence in your knowledge and ability to meet the deadlines.

In our experience, authors have become ill, gotten divorced or married, had a child, changed jobs, moved homes, had lightning strike the house, been flooded, or been the victim of other catastrophes. There is no way to predict that such an event will occur or disrupt work on the chapter. If any event occurs that will cause a delay in your work on the chapter, please advise your primary editor. A coauthor might be found to help you complete the material. If you cannot provide the material in keeping with the deadlines, we will need to either replace you or drop the material from the text. The manuscript cannot be put into production until all chapters are received. One author can hold up, in this book's case, more than fifty others. We ask, therefore, that you keep in close contact with us as the project evolves.

4. Formatting

We have gained some experience in the process of putting together a manuscript and have learned a number of things the hard way, and will do whatever we can so that you do not learn the same lessons the same way.

We have given you a copy of a sample chapter. We would like to follow the same format with inclusion of tips, figures, and cases. Here are the specifics.

A. Audience

The people who will read this book will be primarily attorneys. However, the book has a strong market in expert witnesses, legal nurse consultants, claims adjusters and others. Although practicing nurses may read this book, they are not your primary audience. Therefore, do not write the chapter as if you were advising nurses. As you prepare your chapter, keep these audiences in mind. Your sentences should clearly define the roles of the readers. The tone of the book is professional and avoids directly addressing the reader.

Example: "You should request to see the staffing sheets for the day of the incident" should be reworded as "Both the defense and plaintiff counsel should review the staffing sheets for the day of the incident."

B. Confidentiality
The material we supply to you is confidential. The publishing world is competitive. Please use care in discussing your involvement in this book until it goes into production. Once it is in production, we will be working hard to market and promote the book.

C. Word processor
We ask that you use Microsoft Word rather than any other word processor. Although we have gotten files in Word Perfect form, it is sometimes difficult to convert these files. We cannot use Macintosh files.

D. Outline
Your outline (due March 20, 2012) should be in simple list format. It does not have to be a detailed outline. You are not bound to strictly stick to your outline if, as you prepare your first draft, you recognize the need to add or delete sections. The outline should be sent to us in electronic format.

See Figure 1 for an example of an outline. Most examples in these Authors' Guidelines come from Autopsy Reports, written by Cyril Wecht, M.D., J.D. Steven Koehler, MPH, PhD, and included in Iyer, Levin and Shea, Medical Legal Aspects of Medical Records.

Figure 1: Outline
X.1 Introduction
X.2 Death Investigation System Development
A. The coroner system in England: A brief history
B. The coroner/medical examiners system in early America
X.3 The Death Investigation Systems in Modern America
A. The coroner's death investigation systems
B. The coroners' inquest systems
C. The medical examiners' death investigation system
X.4 The Stages of Death
X.5 Pronouncing and Criteria for Reporting a Death
A. Pronouncing a death
B. Criteria for reporting a death
X.6 The Death Investigation Team
A. Introduction
B. The discovery
C. The first responders
D. The police
E. The death investigation
F. The scene investigation
G. Hospital deaths
H. Special cases
I. Checking the body into the morgue
X.7 The Forensic Pathologist
X.8 Types of Autopsies
A. Pre-autopsy procedures
B. The microscopic examination
C. The forensic toxicological examination
D. Collecting physical evidence from the body
E. Documentation review

X.9 Exhumation of a Body
X.10 Key Components of the Forensic Reports
A.   The pathology report
B.   The death certificate
C.   The cause of death
D.   The mechanism of death
E.   The manner of death
X.11 Definition: Medicolegal
X.12 Summary

E. First draft
   Please note that first draft is not a rough draft. (A rough draft is missing sections of content which you plan to add.) We do not have a rough draft phase in this project. The first draft should conform to these Author Guidelines and the publisher's guidelines to make it possible to easily make changes in the manuscript for the final draft. All files are electronically submitted to your primary editor. The editors (Barbara and Pat) will give you feedback on the first draft in preparation for finalizing the manuscript for the final draft. The sooner you send the first draft, the better in terms of getting you timely feedback. Barbara and Pat will be reading forty-five or more chapters and always appreciate the early birds!

F. Manuscript preparation
The following guidelines apply to your manuscript.

1. Headers
Headers are the words in bold which identify each of the subsections of the chapter. They make it easy for the reader to locate information. Although we take them

for granted, there are a few important points on their use. Your chapter will probably have two or at the most three levels of headers. Please follow the formatting guidelines below and use them when the first draft is sent to us. This will save hours of work when your manuscript is being finalized.

a. First level header
First level headers are indicated by X.1, X.2 etc. The publisher will replace the X with the final chapter number when all chapters are submitted. All major words in the first level header are capitalized. The first sentence below the header is flush left. All other paragraphs below the first one are tabbed over. A first level header would look like this:
X.1 The Reason we Do What We Do

b. Second level header
The second level header begins with A., B., etc. Only the first word of the second level header is capitalized. The first sentence below the header is flush left. All other paragraphs below the first one are tabbed over. A second level head would look like this:
A.   Psychology of childrearing

c. Third level header
The third level header is tabbed over one space. It begins with 1., 2., etc. Only the first word of the third level header is capitalized.

The first sentence below the third level header is tabbed over to fit below the beginning of the header. All paragraphs below the first one are tabbed over. A third

level header would look like this:
   1. Importance of fathers on child development

d. Fourth level header
   If you need to use a fourth level header, tab over one space and begin with a. (The four headers above this sentence are fourth level headers.) Type the header (capitalizing the first word only). The first sentence below the fourth level header is tabbed over to fit below the beginning of the header. All paragraphs below the first one are tabbed over.

Figure 2 is an example of the formatting of four levels of headers. Note that a blank line is above each header. There are no blank lines between paragraphs. You'll note that these Authors' Guidelines also use properly set up headers.

Figure 2 Section of a chapter that includes four levels of headers
X.3 The Death Investigation Systems in Modern America (first level header)
Each year approximately 20 percent of the approximately two million people who die in the U.S. undergo a postmortem examination. This examination will take place in either a coroner's office or at a medical examiner's office, dictated by the jurisdiction in which the body was pronounced. The type of death investigation system varies from municipality to municipality and from state to state. America is divided into over 2,000 separate jurisdictions with responsibility for investigating unnatural deaths.

A 2002 survey of the medical legal investigative system in America found that twenty-two states (including the District of Columbia) have a state medical examiner system, eighteen states have a mixture of medical examiner and coroner's systems; and a total of eleven states have a coroner system; nine of which have county coroners and two have district coroners…

A. The coroner's death investigation systems (second level header)
In states and counties utilizing a coroner as the medico-legal investigator, the coroner must be 18 years of age or older, a United States citizen, and a resident of the county while holding office for at least one year prior to election…

1. The coroners' inquest systems (third level header)
The coroner's office, unlike the Medical Examiner (ME) office, is empowered to conduct a coroner's inquest. An inquest is generally a formal procedure for inquiring into the cause, manner, and circumstances of any death resulting from violence or occurring under conditions which give reason to suspect that the death may have been due to a criminal act or criminal negligence.

a. Circumstances requiring an inquest (fourth level header)
Suspicious circumstances warranting an inquest include…

2. Synopsis

The synopsis is the outline that appears at the top of the content. Figure 1 is an example of the synopsis. The synopsis should exactly match the headers used within the chapter. It is often easiest to do it after the first draft is completed.

3. Figures and tables

A figure is a list of items, a diagram, a medical record form, a photograph, or another visual aid anything that will help the reader understand the concepts better. A table is set up in columns. If you create a figure or table, it should be referred to in the text. It is the publisher's job to place the figure as close to the reference as possible. Each figure should be numbered by you, as shown in the sample chapter. Text-based figures or tables may be placed at the end of the chapter after the summary. The sample chapter has a text based figure at the end of the chapter. Photographs or other graphic figures should be saved as separate files. Do not place the actual figure, table, or graphic illustration within the body of the chapter where they are referred to. They will just have to be moved. If you have quite a bit of content, you may set up an appendix. Appendices might consist of forms, examples of reports, or other lengthy material that would otherwise break up the text.

4. Figure/table list

The first draft of your chapter should include a figure/table list (Figure 3). This is a simple listing of the figures which will help us identify the figures and make sure we have them all. Without the list, it is surprisingly easy to assign the same figure number to more than one figure. Trust me, we've done it.

Figure 3 List of Figures/Tables/Appendix

Figure X.1	Body illustrating dependent lividity
Figure X.2	A forensic pathologist conducting an external examination
Figure X.3	Autopsy Face Sheet/Diagnosis
Figure X.4	The working Death Certificate
Figure X.5	The examination table
Figure X.6	The "Y" incision
Figure X.7	The chest plate and the intestines
Figure X.8	Collecting blood from the heart
Figure X. 9	Collecting bile from the gallbladder
Figure X.10	Removing the brain
Figure X.11	Examination of the heart
Figure X.12	Sewing up the body after the postmortem examination
Figure X.13	The autopsy instruments
Figure X.14	Body fluids
Figure X.15	X-ray of a bullet in the head
Figure X.16	A possible bite-mark on a victim
Figure X.17	Tire marks on the lower leg
Figure X.18	The final autopsy report
Figure X.19	The toxicological report
Appendix X.1	The autopsy protocol
Table X.1	Normal mean weights of the internal organs by sex and age

Table X.2   The therapeutic, toxic, and lethal range of common drugs

This list provides the publisher with the "legend" or the words which will go under your figures. It is also the place to note wording required by sources which have given you permission to reprint material. For example, Figure X.4, Critical care flow sheet, reprinted with permission of Minor Medical Center, Bellevdere, New Hampshire.

5. Endnotes and additional reading
Please refer to the sample chapter for formatting. Citations are to be denoted in the text with brackets [1]. Any material (texts, articles) which were not referred to in the text, but would be helpful to the reader, would be labeled "Additional Reading". As a general rule, it is not a good idea to cite material that is more than five years old, unless the material is classic.

6. Tips
The tips are points that you think are crucial for the audience to understand. Tips are the important concepts which you want to stand out. You need not repeat the content of a tip within the text. Keep the length of the tip confined to no more than two sentences. Anything longer than that gets hard to read. Set off the tip with a blank line above and below the tip.

Figure 4: How tips are noted in the chapter
Tip: The training that a coroner receives may range from absolutely none to a few weeks.

7. Permissions

The general rule of thumb in publishing is that if you quote more than 250 words from one source in one passage, or you use a figure from an article or textbook, or want to reproduce a blank medical record form, you need permission. The exception to needing permission is anything that is considered to be in the public domain (published by the government). Permissions can be time consuming and difficult to obtain, so it would be very helpful to identify any permissions you think you will need at the time you send in the first draft. A manuscript cannot be put into production until the permissions are obtained. We will give you the language to use if you seek permission for reproduction of material. This is a separate file that you can use to personalize the permission. Please send a copy of the permission form to your editor at the same time you send it to the original source.

8. When to Send Your Files

Your files should be emailed to your primary editor. We will need an email with your chapter's files at the time of the first and all subsequent drafts. The electronic file will be used to send the draft to the other coeditor.

Your chapter should be assembled in this order:
Title of chapter, your name
Synopsis (outline)
Content
Figure list
Figures/tables (except any graphic figures which should be saved separately)
Additional reading

At the time of the final draft: one paragraph biography.

9. Viruses
Please practice safe computing. Be sure your computer system has a virus checking program which is routinely updated with new virus definitions. (One of our contributors gave us a virus before we used virus detection software. It took lots of expensive computer consulting time to fix the problem.)

10. Important Requests
- Do not send your chapter by regular mail. (Pat was involved in a project with a coauthor who sent the manuscript to the publisher by US Mail two weeks before Christmas. The package has not surfaced to this day.)
- Ask your primary editor to verify that the file was received. If she does not respond, call her. Email can stop working temporarily. We want to avoid a situation in which you have sent the manuscript and assume it was received, when it was not.
- Keep a copy of your computer files and your paper manuscript at your home or office at the time you send in your manuscript. This will save you much trouble in case your manuscript disappears into a black hole somewhere.
- Make sure whatever computer is used to prepare your manuscript is plugged into a surge protector, and is backed up regularly if you save your manuscript on the hard drive of the computer. (One of our contributors had her hard drive fried in a power surge and her entire

chapter was gone-forever.) Don't let this happen to you.

Thank you again for agreeing to participate in this project.

Pat Iyer and Barbara Levin

Pat Iyer (editor's contact information)
Barbara Levin (editor's contact information)

Building Blocks for a Successful Legal Nurse Consulting Practice

Patricia Iyer, MSN RN LNCC

2013, 185 pages, Softcover

Price: $37.00

Patricia Iyer Associates

Do you want to grow your independent legal nurse consulting business – develop a group of raving fans who will recommend you to their colleagues? One of the essential components of building a strong business is establishing a loyal customer base. This book is directed to legal nurse consultants to help them do just that. The principles here will help you to establish and maintain successful relationships with customers to build a solid business. There is an abundance of opportunity for legal nurse consultants. Learn how to tap into it.

Running a business is a challenge for most entrepreneurs. Are you scrambling for business? This book is geared to the to the legal nurse consultant who is searching for tips to jump start a consulting practice.

Even after you make that client or prospect to become a raving fan for you and your services.

The principles and tips in this book will help you gain success in your legal nurse consulting practice. Patricia Iyer has held nothing back. Learn from a successful legal nurse consultant as you build the foundation of your company.

Chapter 1: The Entrepreneurial Mindset
Chapter 2: Business Development
Chapter 3: Creating Your Website
Chapter 4: Attracting Your Prospects
Chapter 5: Getting Your First and Next Cases
Chapter 6: Turning Prospects into Clients Through Cold Calls and Visits
Chapter 7: Adopting Smart Business Strategies
Chapter 8: Using the Expert Witness Route into the Field of Legal Nurse Consulting

For more information visit our website:
www.patiyer.com

Secrets of Expanding Your Legal Nurse Consulting Business

Patricia Iyer, MSN RN LNCC

2013, 185 pages, Softcover

Price: $37.00

Patricia Iyer Associates

You have set up your independent legal nurse consulting business – you've sent out some mailings, made some cold calls and visits, and gotten varying responses. You wonder, "What else can I do to get business?" This text teaches you advanced secrets of marketing to attorneys. Expand your business with the wealth of ideas in this book, master how you demonstrate your expertise to attorneys. In an environment in which attorneys are bombarded with sales messages, the strategies in this book will set you well ahead of your competitors.

Learn how to share your knowledge with your prospects and clients through a blog on your website, presentations, exhibiting, books, videos, teleseminars and webinars. Have you heard of vlogs and blooks? This book will teach you how to use them.

Harness the power of the ideas in this book to build your legal nurse consulting practice - they work. Patricia Iyer MSN RN LNCC loaded this book with concrete information you can use today. You'll learn what has made her legal nurse consulting business one of the most successful of its kind. Gain from her experiences, grab the ideas that will work for you, and watch your business take off.

Chapter 1: Launch a Blog
Chapter 2: Engaging Your Target Market
Chapter 3: Building Relationships with Time-Tested Tips for Tradeshow Exhibiting
Chapter 4: Using Information to Market a Legal Nurse Consulting Practice
Chapter 5: Exploiting the Power of Video Marketing
Chapter 6: Expanding Your Business Through Teleseminars and Webinars

For more information visit our website:
www.patiyer.com

Honing Your Legal Nurse Consulting Skills

Patricia Iyer, MSN RN LNCC

2013, 180+ pages, softcover

Price: $37.00

Patricia Iyer Associates

There are many legal nurse consultants vying for the business of attorneys. With so many legal nurse consultants to pick from, how do you assure you are the one selected? The short answer is to hone your skills to the point of excellence. The long answer is that there are many aspects of your skills as a legal nurse consulting that you can change. This text looks at some of them, and shares insider information from Patricia Iyer MSN RN LNCC, an experienced and successful legal nurse consultant with 25 years of experience in the field.

In *Honing Legal Nurse Consulting Skills,* you will learn how to put your best foot forward with a polished resume or CV that accurately and professionally presents your credentials. You will learn tips and tricks for organizing printed medical records – both handwritten and computer generated. You will find out how to efficiently organize records that come to you on a disk. The chapter on preparing medical summaries and chronologies shares several techniques for effective report writing. Your work product is the primary way you get and retain clients. Additional chapters will help you determine if a law firm position is right for you, and how to capture the details of a fat paced independent medical examination. The last part of the book explores how to master the challenging role of being an expert witness, with three chapters that cover case intake and analysis, report writing and testifying.

Chapter 1: Polishing Your Resume and Curriculum Vitae
Chapter 2: Organizing Medical Records
Chapter 3: Summarizing Medical Records
Chapter 4: Proving Your Value as an Inhouse Legal Nurse Consultant
Chapter 5: Observing as an LNC at an Independent Medical Examination
Chapter 6: Mastering the Expert Witness Role
Chapter 7: Crafting Expert Witness Reports
Chapter 8: Learning Testifying Strategies

For more information visit our website:
www.patiyer.com

[1] http://writing.wisc.edu/Handbook/CommonErrors_BestMod.html
[2] Rooks, S. *Punctuate Like a Pro!* Ebook
[3] Id
[4] Id
[5] Oettle, K. *Making Your Point: A Practical Guide to Persuasive Legal Writing*, ALM Publishing, 2007
[6] Truss, L. *Eats, Shoots & Leaves*, Gotham Books, 2006
[7] See Oettle
[8] See Rooks
[9] Id
[10] Id
[11] *Franklin Covey Style Guide*, Franklin Covey, 1999
[12] Id
[13] Id

Made in the USA
Charleston, SC
28 January 2014